WRESTLING STRENGTH

PREPARE TO WIN

Matt Brzycki

D1232996

a RAM Publishing Pruduction
Blue River Press, Indianapolis, Indiana

Wrestling Strength: Prepare to Win © 2002 Matt Brzycki

LCCN: 2002091010

Cover designed by Phil Velikan
Cover photography provided by Lanny Bryant, *Wrestling USA* magazine

Printed in the United States of America
10 9 8 7 6 5 4 3 2 1

Distributed in the United States by
Cardinal Publishers Group
7301 Georgetown Road, Suite 118
Indianapolis, Indiana 46268
www.cardinalpub.com

TABLE OF CONTENTS

PREFACE

From February 1986-May 2001, I have had nearly 60 articles featured in *Wrestling USA* magazine. I would like to thank Lanny Bryant and his family for publishing those articles in their magazine and granting permission to allow them to be compiled in book form.

The articles were written over the course of more than 15 years, the earliest appearing in the February 15, 1986 issue. I have done some editing of the articles for this book to "standardize" the changes in my style of writing that have occurred over this lengthy period of time. Actually, all of the articles that I wrote prior to 1991 were done on a typewriter. As you might imagine, it was quite painstaking to make any changes to the text. In fact, making the smallest of changes required retyping sections of the article or, in some cases, the entire article. Needless to say, the texts of those early articles were essentially rough "first drafts" and I have used this opportunity to make belated edits.

Though I never competed as a wrestler, the sport of wrestling has given me a wealth of fond memories. My earliest recollection dates back to when I was a young teen who marveled at — and was inspired by — the renowned physical training of the great Dan Gable as he prepared for the 1972 Olympics in Munich. Another memory that I have of wrestlers is from 1978. At the time, I was a 21-year-old Drill Instructor at the Marine Corps Recruit Depot in San Diego, California. As part of their training, recruits had to maneuver through an obstacle course that consisted of numerous poles, logs, beams and hurdles and ended with a rope climb. Negotiating the obstacle course in a speedy fashion requires a high degree of strength, balance, agility and determination. As motivation, recruits were timed in their efforts and a record was kept for the best-ever time. Every now and then, a recruit would break the all-time record by a half second or so. One day, word quickly spread about a recruit who broke the record for the obstacle course by an unbelievable two seconds. The depot newspaper ran an article about the recruit who set the new record — an unusually large individual who had gone to college on a football scholarship and later joined the Marines. To make a long story short, the recruit was Greg Gibson. He went on to become a three-time world silver medalist in freestyle wrestling from 1981-83 and the 1984 Olympic silver medalist in Greco-Roman wrestling. (At the time of this writing, Greg is a Master Sergeant in the Marine Corps and assistant coach of their wrestling team.) In 1981 as an undergraduate student at Penn State, I participated in a wrestling class taught by the legendary Bill Koll who was a three-time NCAA champion for Northern Iowa (1946-48) and twice won the award as the outstanding wrestler in the tournament (1947-48). Despite his age, we still dreaded having him demonstrate moves on us. Among other things, we did not want to be on the wrong end of a cross face.

Of all the different sports with which I have worked over the years, I have been with wrestling the longest and on the most regular basis. Since September 1982, I have been involved in the strength and conditioning of collegiate wrestlers at three different schools: Penn State, Princeton University and Rutgers University. Over this period of time, I have met a great number of wrestlers and coaches who have meant much to me both professionally as well as personally. From a professional standpoint, I have had the opportunity to work with two of the all-time coaching greats in the history of collegiate wrestling: John Johnston of Princeton and Deane Oliver of Rutgers — both of whom were head coaches at the collegiate level for a total of more than a half century (and they themselves were accomplished collegiate wrestlers as well). In addition, I have worked with hundreds of their wrestlers (and those of John Johnston's two very capable coaching successors, Eric Pearson and Michael

New) who are far too numerous to mention. From a personal standpoint, the best man at my wedding was Andy Foltiny who wrestled for Rutgers in the late 1970s (captaining the team as a senior) and then served as an assistant wrestling coach at the school for more than a decade. Andy was also my training partner from 1985-90 and, pound-for-pound, was one of the strongest men that I have ever seen. And several years ago, Tom O'Rourke — another exceptionally strong individual who wrestled for Andy at Rutgers (also captaining the team as a senior) — asked me to be the godfather of his daughter, Kathleen.

Wrestlers quickly gained my utmost respect primarily because of their warrior-like nature. Like true warriors, wrestlers are generally fierce, relentless, intense, aggressive, dedicated, resourceful and purposeful to a degree that separates them from most others. Boxers, judo players and the various martial artists are also true warriors. Unfortunately, the fact of the matter is that the warrior is a vanishing breed.

As a sport, you cannot get much more basic than wrestling. There is really no equipment except for the uniform — and there is very little of that. There are no implements or apparatus. It is just a wrestler and an opponent. Two warriors. One goal.

This book is dedicated to wrestlers and the warrior lifestyle.

Matt Brzycki
May 2, 2002

Chapter 1

STRENGTH TRAINING:
SET YOUR PRIORITIES!

Over the years, I have often been asked questions like "How can I get my abs ripped?" or "What can I do to get my arms bigger?" or "How can I set the school record in the bench press?" Unfortunately, these questions are sometimes asked by athletes who are involved in a variety of sports. Questions such as these tell me that the athletes really do not have their priorities straight — they are more concerned with improving their physical appearance and weight-room notoriety than improving their athletic potential. You can certainly make the argument that "Well, if I look better then I'll feel better about myself. I'll be more confident on the mat and be a better wrestler." Maybe so but you could look like Tarzan and still wrestle like Cheetah. Remember, too, that the winner of a wrestling match is never decided by a posedown or a bench-press contest.

PRIORITIES

There are two main reasons why wrestlers should lift weights: To reduce their risk of injury and to increase their potential for improved performance.

Reduce Injury Potential

As a wrestler, your primary purpose in lifting weights is to reduce your risk of injury. During the 1997-98 season, data collected by the NCAA Injury Surveillance System revealed that wrestlers had a higher injury rate during practices than all but two other athletes: football players (in the spring) and female gymnasts. During actual competition, wrestlers had the highest injury rate of any athletes other than football players. Also, 39% of all injuries sustained by wrestlers were severe enough to restrict or miss participation for 7 or more days and 6.1% of all injuries required surgery.

If you get injured and cannot compete, you are not doing your team any good. Perhaps your team will lose a meet because you were unable to wrestle and had to forfeit your match. And it is not doing you any good, either, especially if you are a high school wrestler hoping to earn an athletic scholarship. Imagine a college coach showing up to watch your match and being told that you would not be wrestling because you are injured. The college coach might have second thoughts about offering you a scholarship.

By increasing the strength of your muscles, bones and connective tissue, these structures can tolerate more stress; if these structures can tolerate more stress, you will be less susceptible to injury. This does not mean that if you increase your strength you will never get hurt. Many injuries are the result of being in the wrong place at the wrong time. However, being stronger will certainly reduce your risk. In addition, stronger biological tissue will reduce the severity of any injuries that you may get and allow you to return from injury sooner.

The areas that should receive the most emphasis are the ones most likely to get injured in wrestling: the neck, shoulder and knee. Other areas of priority should be the lower back, elbow and ankle.

Increase Performance Potential

A second important reason for improving your strength is to increase your performance potential as an athlete. "Potential" is the key word here. If you lift weights, it does not mean that you will automatically become a better wrestler. By increasing the strength of your muscles, you will be able to produce more force. If you can produce more force, you will have the *potential* to perform your techniques more efficiently — that is, with less effort — provided that you have practiced your wrestling skills so that you know how to apply that force in a sport-specific fashion.

When you work on your skills, you must practice them in the exact manner as you would do them on the mat. Practice makes perfect . . . but only if you practice perfect. If you practice sloppy then your skills will be sloppy.

BETTER QUESTIONS

So questions that would indicate you have your priorities in order as a wrestler might be "What's the best way to strengthen my neck to prevent injury?" or "What can I do to become a better conditioned wrestler?" or "How can I improve my functional strength on the mat?"

Actually, there's a simple question that you can ask yourself to determine if your priorities are straight: "Am I a wrestler who lifts weights or a weightlifter who wrestles?"

Chapter 2

INJURY TRENDS IN WRESTLING

In 1982, the NCAA developed its Injury Surveillance System (ISS) to provide data on injury trends in intercollegiate athletics. Each year, injury data are collected from a representative sample of NCAA member institutions. The resulting data summaries are then reviewed by the NCAA Committee on Competitive Safeguards and Medical Aspects of Sports. The committee then suggests changes in rules, protective equipment or coaching techniques to reduce the injury rates.

Although the data on injuries were gathered from collegiate wrestlers, the information is still quite applicable and useful to high school coaches and athletes.

SUMMARY OF THE WRESTLING DATA

During the 1997-98 season, data on wrestling injuries were collected from 53 NCAA schools: 20 from Division I (D-1), 18 from Division II (D-2) and 15 from Division III (D-3). What follows is a brief overview of the data from that season (unless otherwise noted) along with my comments as it applies to strength and conditioning.

Practice Injury Rates

Data: The highest rate of injuries in practice occurred at D-3 schools followed by D-1 and D-2, respectively. Actually, this was the fourth season in a row that the D-3 schools had the highest practice injury rates.

Comment: None.

Match Injury Rates

Data: D-3 schools also had the highest rate of injuries in matches followed by D-1 and D-2, respectively. This was the fourth season out of the last five that D-3 schools had the highest match injury rates.

Comment: None.

Pre-, Regular and Post-Season Injury Rates

Data: Injury rates were highest during the pre-season followed by the regular season and the post-season. This was the sixth year in a row that this occurred.

Comment: In my opinion, conditioning is a factor here. Like most competitive athletes, wrestlers tend to be in better condition during the season than prior to it. The relatively high incidence of injuries during the pre-season can be attributed to poor conditioning. I think that the lower injury rate during the post-season is related to the fact that the wrestlers are more evenly matched in terms of skill, strength and conditioning. Generally speaking, wrestlers who qualify for post-season competition also have the highest levels of skill, strength and conditioning.

Home and Away Injury Rates

Data: There is no information available concerning home and away injuries beyond the 1995-96 season. In the eight seasons that this has been reported upon — that is, from 1988-89 to 1995-96 — the injury rates were higher when wrestling away compared to wrestling at home in all but one season (1994-95).

Comment: In general, I think that competing "on the road" makes an athlete less aggressive than when competing at home — due to fatigue from traveling, anxiety related to unfriendly fans and unfamiliar surroundings — thereby increasing the likelihood of injury. In effect, you have an "away" wrestler who is more passive than usual competing against a "home" wrestler who is more aggressive than usual.

Injuries by Weight Class

Data: The percent of all injuries by weight class were 118 (7%), 126 (9%), 134 (11%), 142 (10%), 150 (12%), 158 (10%), 167 (11%), 177 (10%), 190 (11%) and heavyweight (9%).

Comment: Interestingly, the percentage of injuries was very consistent among all weight classes — 7 of the 10 were between 10-12% and 9 of the 10 were between 9-12%. I suspect that the slightly lower percentage of injuries in the extreme weight classes — that is, 118, 126 and heavyweight — was due to the fact that there are relatively few wrestlers competing at those weights.

Injuries by School Year

Data: The percent of all injuries by school year were freshman (32.0%), sophomore (28.5%), junior (22.63%), senior (12.86%) and fifth year (4.0%).

Comment: At first glance, it is tempting to speculate that younger wrestlers are more prone to injury because they are less physically mature than their veteran counterparts. While this may have some truth, keep in mind that the greatest number of competitors is from the freshman and sophomore classes. Very few athletes wrestle during all four years of college. Indeed, they may compete during their first one or two years of college but not during their final years. No doubt, the main reason why fifth-year athletes had such a low percentage of injuries is that there are relatively few who wrestle that long.

Practice and Match Injury Rates

Data: The data show that the injury rate during matches was more than four times that of practices which is roughly the average for the past 13 seasons. (Note: The total number of injuries was greater during practices but so were the number of exposures.)

Comment: I believe that the higher injury rates during matches is a result of both wrestlers competing with a continuous, all-out effort as compared to practices in which there are certainly all-out efforts but not as sustained. If so, the potential for injury can be reduced by being as highly conditioned as possible. This will allow wrestlers to put forth greater all-out efforts for longer periods of time.

Injury Rates by Period

Data: During matches, most of the injuries occurred in the second period (39.23%) followed by the third period (36.98%) and the first period (22.19%). One injury was reported during the warm-up and no injuries were reported during overtime periods. (Four injuries were classified as "other.")

14

Comment: I think that conditioning played a role here as well. As fatigue becomes a factor, athletes are more susceptible to injury — particularly if their opponents have shown little signs of exhaustion. I suspect that the low number of injuries in the third period is because some matches do not go the distance.

Activity When Injured

Data: Most of the injuries in both practices and matches occurred during a takedown (42.07%). Other activities in which injuries were sustained included sparring (22.47%), riding (9.24%), an escape (5.74%), a reversal (5.49%) and a near fall (4.00%).

Comment: No real surprises here. The top two activities that result in the most injuries — namely takedowns and sparring — are when both wrestlers are on the offensive.

Position When Injured

Data: The majority of the injuries in both practices and matches occurred in the neutral position (51.28%) followed by the "bottom" position (33.11%) and the "top" position (9.56%).

Comment: Again, this would be expected. Both wrestlers are on the offensive in the neutral position (and it is also when takedowns and sparring — the top two injury-producing activities — are performed).

New Versus Recurring Injury

Data: The overwhelming majority of the injuries sustained by wrestlers in practices and matches were new ones (80.98%). Recurring injuries from the current season and the previous season that were sustained during practices and matches accounted for 6.44% and 10.60%, respectively.

Comment: No comment other than the fact that this underscores the importance of rehabilitating injuries appropriately and adequately before resumption of wrestling activities so that the risk of experiencing a recurring injury is reduced.

Time Loss Injury Summary

Data: In terms of time lost from training, 30.0% of all injuries resulted in a loss of 1-2 days, 32.0% a loss of 3-6 days, 14.6% a loss of 7-9 days and 23.2% a loss of 10 days or more. These numbers are very close to the 13-year averages which are as follows: 29.9% of all injuries resulted in a loss of 1-2 days, 32.1% a loss of 3-6 days, 12.2% a loss of 7-9 days and 25.7% a loss of 10 or more days. This was the tenth time in eleven years in which the highest percentage of injuries resulted in a loss of 3-6 days of training; it was the thirteenth year in a row in which the lowest percentage of injuries resulted in a loss of 7-9 days of training.

Comment: No comment except that it is very fortunate that more than 60% of all injuries only resulted in a loss of training of less than one week.

Injuries Requiring Surgery

Data: Surgery was required in 0.7% of all injuries. Injuries requiring surgery were highest during the season (0.5% of all injuries) and lowest during the post-season (0.2% of all injuries) — a trend that has been the same for the past 13 seasons.

Comment: It is my opinion that the lower percentage of injuries that require surgery during the post-season is related to competition between wrestlers who are more evenly matched in terms of skill, strength and conditioning.

Injury Involvement

Data: Most of the injuries sustained in practices and matches involved contact with another wrestler (51.65%). The second greatest number of injuries was incurred from contact with the mat (22.53%). A significant number of injuries (17.49%) were sustained without any apparent contact of any kind — such as rotation with the foot planted.

Comment: None.

Top Three Body Parts Injured

Data: Of the 973 injuries reported, the top three body parts injured were the knee (20%), shoulder (13%) and ankle (7%). In fact, the knee and shoulder have been the top two body parts injured every year since 1985-86. The ankle has been the third most frequently injured body part in all but three of the past thirteen seasons — the others being the head (once) and face (twice). It should be noted that the next four body parts most frequently injured during the 1997-98 season were the head, elbow, neck and lower back.

Comment: It is obvious that the body parts that are most frequently injured while wrestling should be emphasized in a strength and conditioning program. Specifically, exercises should be done regularly to target the knee (e.g., leg press, leg curl, leg extension), shoulder (e.g., multiple-joint "pushing" and "pulling" movements, internal/external rotation), ankle (e.g., calf raise, dorsi flexion), elbow (e.g., bicep curl, tricep extension), neck (e.g., neck flexion, neck extension, lateral flexion, shoulder shrug) and lower back (back extension).

Top Three Types of Injury

Data: Of the 973 injuries reported, the top three types of injuries were sprains (29%), strains (17%) and infection (15%). Sprains have actually been the most frequently reported injury every season since 1985-86 (13 seasons) while either strains or infections has been either the second or third most frequently reported injury every year since 1986-87. (In 1985-86, strains and contusions ranked number two and three, respectively.)

Comment: These data underscore the importance of strengthening the muscles and connective tissue that surround joints as a precautionary measure against sprains and strains. Stronger biological tissue can tolerate greater stress which reduces the potential for injury.

Comparison to Other Sports

Data: During the 1997-98 season, data collected by the NCAA ISS revealed that wrestlers had a higher injury rate during practices than all but two other types of athletes: football players (in the spring) and female gymnasts. During actual competition, wrestlers had the highest injury rate of any athletes other than football players. Also, 39% of all injuries sustained by wrestlers were severe enough to restrict or miss participation for seven or more days and 6.1% of all injuries required surgery.

Comment: The risk of sustaining an injury while wrestling is a grim reality.

BE PREPARED!

Strength and conditioning for wrestling should be a year-round endeavor — not just immediately prior to the season. Further, it is extremely critical that wrestlers engage in strength and conditioning activities during the season since this is the time when they need to be as strong and as highly conditioned as possible. Engaging in strength and conditioning activities throughout the year will also help wrestlers stay at or near their competitive bodyweights. Finally, athletes should practice proper wrestling technique thousands and thousands of times. The skills should be practiced perfectly and exactly as how they would be used in competition.

What can wrestlers do to reduce their risk of injury? It all comes down to being prepared.

Chapter **3**
PROTECTING THE KNEE

According to the NCAA's Injury Surveillance System, the knee has been one of the top two most often injured body parts in wrestling (the other being the shoulder). Moreover, the knee is the most common site of injury that requires surgery. Increasing the strength of the muscles surrounding your knees can lower your risk of sustaining an injury while wrestling. In addition, several precautions and guidelines can be used to ensure that the strength-training program itself does not predispose you to a knee injury and is as productive as possible.

THE KNEE JOINT

Technically known as a "diarthrodial hinge joint," the knee is the largest and most complicated joint in your body. The knee joint has three articulations (or points where bones are in contact): two tibiofemoral joints and the patellofemoral joint. The former is an articulation of your tibia (the large bone in your lower leg) and femur (the large bone in your upper leg); the latter of your patella (your kneecap) and femur.

Various tendons, ligaments and cartilages support and protect the knee. These connective tissues include the patellar tendon, collateral ligaments (medial and lateral), cruciate ligaments (anterior and posterior) and menisci (medial and lateral).

MUSCLES OF THE KNEE

Twelve muscles influence your knee joint, primarily your hamstring and quadricep groups (which account for a total of 7 of the 12 muscles).

Hamstrings

Your hamstrings or "hams" are located on the backside of your upper leg and actually include three separate muscles: the semitendinous, semimembranosus and biceps femoris. Together, these muscles are involved in flexing (or bending) your lower leg around your knee joint (raising your heel toward your buttocks) and in hip extension.

Quadriceps

Your quadriceps or "quads" are the most important muscles on the front part of your thighs. As the name suggests, the quadriceps are made up of four muscles. The vastus lateralis is located on the outside of your thigh; the vastus medialis resides on the inner (medial) side of your thigh above your patella; between these two thigh muscles is the vastus intermedius; and, finally, laying on top of the vastus intermedius is the rectus femoris. The main function of your quads is extending (or straightening) your lower leg at the knee joint.

KNEE EXERCISES

Multiple-joint movements for the lower body — such as the deadlift, squat and leg press — are important because they address a large amount of muscle mass, including the hamstrings and quadriceps. The best way to provide direct stimulation for these muscles, however, is to perform single-joint or isolation movements. There are two main single-joint movements that can be used to isolate the hamstrings and quadriceps using conventional equipment:

1. **Leg curl**. This is the best movement for isolating your hamstrings. You can perform this exercise sitting, standing or laying prone using a machine (either selectorized or plate-loaded) or manual resistance.

2. **Leg Extension**. You can isolate your quadriceps with this movement. This exercise can be done on a machine (either selectorized or plate-loaded) or with manual resistance.

GUIDELINES AND PRECAUTIONS

Sometimes the strength-training program is the genesis of knee problems and may actually predispose you to an injury. The following precautionary measures can lower that risk while making your workouts more productive:

1. Perform 1-2 multiple-joint movements for your lower body 2-3 times per week. Multiple-joint movements incorporate an integrated effort of several major muscles.

2. Avoid doing "full" squats with a barbell. If you prefer to do this movement, do not squat down to a point where your hips are near your ankles. Squatting this deeply increases the stress placed upon the knee ligaments and cartilage. If you do barbell squats, limit your range of motion such that in the bottom position your upper legs are roughly parallel to the ground. Remember, too, that barbell squats are contraindicated for those with low-back pain.

3. Do single-joint exercises for your hamstrings and quadriceps. Only through single-joint movements can these muscles be targeted directly.

4. Do exercises for your hip area before those for your hamstrings and quadriceps. Here's why: Multiple-joint movements require the use of smaller, weaker muscles to assist in the exercise. (As a rule of thumb, the legs are the weak link when performing multiple-joint movements for the hips and the arms are the weak link when performing multiple-joint movements for the upper body.) If you fatigue your smaller muscles first — in this case, your hamstrings and quadriceps — you will weaken an already weak link. As a result, you will limit the workload placed on the larger, more powerful muscles of your hip region and restrict the potential for their development.

5. Provide equal attention to your hamstrings and quadriceps. These muscles — as well as all others in your body — are arranged in such a way that they perform oppos-

ing functions: Your hamstrings flex your lower leg and your quadriceps extend your lower leg. When one muscle acts in opposition to another, it is referred to as an "antagonist." It is important to provide antagonistic partnerships with an equal — or nearly equal — amount of work so that there is not a muscular imbalance between the two areas. In particular, the hamstrings are very susceptible to pulls and tears. Strong hamstrings are necessary to balance the effects of the powerful quadricep muscles. Therefore, you should perform approximately the same volume — that is, frequency of training, number of exercises, sets and repetitions — for your hamstrings as you do for your quadriceps.

In this way, you will (1) target the two major muscles that affect your knee joint — your hamstrings and quadriceps — in a direct and balanced manner; (2) avoid overtraining your quadriceps (assuming that other exercises in your program offer a minimal amount of indirect work for that muscle); and, most importantly, (3) protect your knees against injury.

Chapter 4

PROTECTING THE SHOULDER

According to the NCAA's Injury Surveillance System, the shoulder has a long history of being one of the top two most frequently injured body parts in wrestling (the other being the knee). Increasing the strength of your shoulders can reduce your risk of incurring an injury while wrestling. In addition, several precautions can be taken to ensure that the strength-training program itself does not predispose you to a shoulder injury.

THE SHOULDER COMPLEX

The so-called "shoulder complex" consists of the shoulder joint — technically known as the "glenohumeral joint" — and the shoulder girdle. The former structure is a typical ball-and-socket joint, formed by the union of the round head of your upper arm (the "ball") and the shallow cavity of your shoulder blade (the "socket"). The extensive mobility offered by this skeletal arrangement allows a wide variety of movements over a considerable range of motion. But what the shoulder complex provides in mobility, it sacrifices in stability. These two factors — namely mobility and instability — make the shoulder complex quite prone to a host of injuries.

THE SHOULDER MUSCLES

Although the ligaments of your shoulder joint do not furnish much in the way of stability, the muscles crossing and covering the joint provide added strength. The primary muscles of your shoulders are the deltoids, the so-called "rotator cuff" and the trapezius.

Deltoids

Your deltoids or "delts" are actually composed of three separate parts or "heads." The anterior deltoid is found on the front of your shoulder and is used to raise your upper arm forward; the middle deltoid is found on the side of your shoulder and is involved when you lift your upper arm sideways (away from your body); the posterior deltoid resides on the back of your shoulder and is used to draw your upper arm backward.

Rotator Cuff

Several deep muscles of the shoulder are often referred to as the "rotator cuff." This functional unit includes the "internal rotators" (the subscapularis and the teres major) and the "external rotators" (the infraspinatus and the teres minor). In addition to performing rotation, these muscles stabilize the shoulder joint against subluxation and prevent shoulder-impingement syndrome (which is a general term that is used to describe a number of problems including bursitis and bicipital tendinitis).

Trapezius

Your trapezius is a kite-shaped (or trapezoid-shaped) muscle that covers the uppermost region of your back and the posterior section of your neck. The primary functions of your "traps" are to elevate your shoulders (as in shrugging), to adduct your scapulae (pinch your shoulder blades together) and to extend your head backward. The trapezius is often considered part of the neck musculature.

SHOULDER EXERCISES

This is a list of the most popular exercises that can be performed to directly strengthen the muscles of your shoulders using conventional equipment:

1. **Front raise**. This is the best exercise for isolating your anterior deltoid. You can perform this movement with dumbbells or manual resistance.

2. **Lateral raise**. You can exercise your middle deltoid with this movement. It can be done with dumbbells, a machine (selectorized or plate-loaded) or manual resistance.

3. **Posterior raise**. This movement is best for exercising your posterior deltoid. You can do this exercise with dumbbells or manual resistance.

4. **Seated press**. This multiple-joint movement involves your anterior deltoid and your triceps. It can be performed with a barbell, dumbbells, trap bar, machines (selectorized and plate-loaded) or manual resistance.

5. **Internal rotation**. This exercise is best for isolating your internal rotators. You can do this movement with dumbbells or manual resistance.

6. **External rotation**. This movement is best for isolating your external rotators. It can be done with dumbbells or manual resistance.

7. **Shoulder shrug**. You can effectively isolate your trapezius (upper fibers) with this exercise. It can be performed with a barbell, dumbbells, trap bar or machines (selectorized and plate-loaded).

8. **Scapulae adduction**. This exercise also involves your trapezius (middle fibers). You can do this movement with a barbell, dumbbells or machines (selectorized and plate-loaded).

9. **Upright row**. This multiple-joint movement involves your trapezius, biceps and lower arms. It can be performed with a barbell, dumbbells, machines (selectorized and plate-loaded) or manual resistance.

GUIDELINES AND PRECAUTIONS

Sometimes the strength-training program is the genesis of shoulder problems and may actually predispose you to an injury. The following precautionary measures can lower that risk:

1. Refrain from doing exercises in which the bar travels behind your head thereby creating shoulder pain. Some individuals may find it difficult — or even impossible — to perform pain-free exercises in which they push or pull the bar behind their heads such as doing the behind-the-neck seated press or lat pulldown. In fact, this position

may exacerbate shoulder-impingement syndrome. Simply doing those same two exercises with the bar positioned in front of your face (rather than behind your head) will reduce the orthopedic stress in your shoulder area. This is not to say that exercising with the bar behind your head cannot be done. Rather, exercising with the bar behind your head should not be performed if it cannot be done in a pain-free manner.

2. Do only a few movements in each workout to directly address your shoulder region. Although there are a wide variety of exercises that you can do to strengthen your shoulders, it is not necessary to do all of them every time that you work out. Doing more than a few exercises for your shoulders in any given workout on a regular basis can eventually lead to overtraining or, worse, an overuse injury.

3. Avoid overworking your anterior deltoid. Most individuals perform far too many exercises that involve the front part of their shoulders. Of the nine shoulder exercises that have been previously mentioned, the front raise and seated press directly address the anterior deltoid. However, a number of other movements involve the anterior deltoid indirectly. For example, the bench press is primarily an exercise for the pectoral muscles of the chest but it also provides indirect work for the anterior deltoid (as well as the triceps). Other movements that indirectly involve the anterior deltoid include the incline press, decline press, dip and bent-arm fly (or "pec dec"). If your training involves much indirect work for your anterior deltoid, you should keep the direct work to a minimum.

4. Provide equal attention to muscles that oppose each other. Your muscles are arranged in your body in such a way that they perform opposing functions. As an example, your anterior deltoid raises your upper arm forward and your posterior deltoid draws your upper arm backward. When one muscle acts in opposition to another, it is referred to as an "antagonist." It is important to provide antagonistic partnerships with an equal — or

nearly equal — amount of work so that there is not a muscular imbalance between the two areas. Therefore, you should perform approximately the same volume — that is, frequency of training, number of exercises, sets and repetitions — for the posterior muscles of your shoulders as the anterior muscles.

In linking these last three points, let's suppose that your training targets your shoulder region three times per week. Furthermore, you prefer to do three exercises during each workout for your shoulders. That said, your three weekly shoulder routines could look like this:

Monday: front raise, lateral raise, posterior raise
Wednesday: internal rotation, external rotation, seated press
Friday: shoulder shrug, upright row, scapulae adduction

In this way, you will (1) target all of the major muscles of your shoulders in a balanced manner; (2) avoid overtraining your anterior deltoid (assuming that other exercises in your program offer a minimal amount of indirect work for that muscle); (3) provide a great deal of variety in your workouts; and, most importantly, (4) protect your shoulders against injury.

Chapter 5

REHABILITATIVE STRENGTH TRAINING

As much as coaches prepare their athletes for the rigors of wrestling, injuries sustained during practices and competition are still an unforeseen and inevitable occurrence. A coach may also have wrestlers who have various "non-contact" injuries such as tendinitis, bursitis, general soreness or other nagging afflictions. Once an athlete is injured, the injured area is usually treated by one or more qualified sportsmedical personnel — such as athletic trainers, physical therapists and so on. In many instances, however, the wrestler eliminates all strength-training exercises — even those that involve uninjured body parts. Discontinuing an entire strength-training program — or even part of it — is not desirable, especially during the season. In fact, some research has shown that a muscle begins to lose size and strength if it is not exercised within about 48-96 hours of its previous workout. Moreover, the rate of strength loss is most rapid during the first few weeks.

OPTIONS AND ADJUSTMENTS

There are several different exercise options and program adjustments that can be used by someone who wants to continue strength training an injured body part. It should be noted that these methods are intended for those injuries that are not viewed as being very serious or extremely painful. As such, it is recommended that an athlete receive approval from a certified sportsmedical authority before initiating any rehabilitative strength training.

Lighten the Resistance

The first step for someone who wants to continue training an injured body part is to reduce the amount of weight being used. This is usually the easiest and most straightforward recommendation. Let's suppose that a wrestler's patellar tendon hurts when doing a leg extension with the normal training weight. Reducing the amount of weight will produce less stress on the tendon and perhaps allow the athlete to perform the exercise in a pain-free manner. The amount that the weight is reduced will depend upon the extent and the nature of an individual's injury.

Reduce the Speed of Movement

If pain-free exercise is still not possible even after reducing the amount of weight, an athlete's next move would be to slow down the speed of movement. This may involve raising the weight in about 4-8 seconds instead of the traditional 1-2 seconds. Reducing the speed of movement will decrease the amount of stress placed on a given joint. Slowing down the speed of movement will also necessitate using a reduced amount of weight thereby decreasing the stress even further.

Change the Exercise Angle

If pain persists during certain exercises involving an injured body part, another adjustment would be to change the angle at which the movement is performed. This option can be used with many exercises for the upper body — especially those that involve the shoulder joint. Let's say that you have a wrestler who has slight shoulder pain when doing a regular supine bench press. In some cases, if the angle of the bench is changed to either an incline or a decline there will be less stress on the shoulder joint. Likewise, some people experience pain when performing a seated press with the bar positioned behind the head. The pain is usually alleviated when performing a seated press with the bar in front of the head.

Another exercise that may exacerbate shoulder pain is a behind-the-neck lat pulldown with an overhand grip. Often, the pain is characterized as a "tightness" or "pinching" in the shoulder joint. Generally, the discomfort can be lessened by changing the angle of the pull. This is accomplished by grasping the bar with the palms facing the torso and pulling the bar to the upper chest instead of behind the neck.

Use a Different Grip

In the case of the shoulder joint, many times there is less stress if a different grip is used. Again, let's say that an athlete has slight pain when doing an exercise such as a bench press. It is quite possible that there will be a significant reduction in pain by simply changing the grip from that used with a barbell to a parallel grip using dumbbells. It should be noted that any exercise that can be performed with a barbell can be performed with dumbbells. These exercises include the bench press, incline press, decline press, seated press, upright row, shoulder shrug, bent-over row, bicep curl and tricep extension. As such, an athlete has an option for varying the grip used in movements for just about every major muscle group in the upper torso.

Perform Different Exercises

Yet another option is to perform different exercises that use the same muscle groups. For instance, if a wrestler simply cannot perform a lat pulldown without experiencing pain or discomfort then perhaps a different exercise can be prescribed that works the same muscles in a pain-free manner. In this case, a seated row or a bent-over row can be substituted to involve the same muscles as a lat pulldown, namely the upper back ("lats"), biceps and forearms.

Limit the Range of Motion

There is a distinct possibility that pain occurs only at certain points in the range of motion (ROM) such as the starting or the mid-range position of the movement. In either case, an athlete can restrict that exercise's ROM. For example, an injury such as a hyperextended elbow or knee is especially painful at the beginning (or stretched position) of a movement. In this instance, the athlete should be instructed not to lower the weight all the way down; similarly, if pain occurs at the mid-range position of an exercise, then the athlete should stop short of full muscular contraction (e.g., flexion or extension). As the injured area heals over a period of time, the athlete can gradually increase the exercise's ROM until a full, pain-free ROM is obtained.

Exercise the Good Limb

If all else fails, an athlete can still exercise the unaffected limb. For example, suppose a wrestler had knee surgery and, as a result, the left leg was placed in a cast from the mid-thigh to the ankle. Obviously, the athlete would not be able to perform any exercises below the left hip joint. However, that athlete should still be able to strength train the muscles on the right side of the lower body. As a matter of fact, some research has shown that training one side of the body will actually affect the muscles on the other side of the body! Researchers are not exactly sure why this occurs but the fact of the matter is that it does occur. This phenomenon has been dubbed as "indirect transfer" or "cross transfer."

Exercise Unaffected Body Parts

This suggestion may seem rather obvious but I have seen enough situations to know that this is not the case. There is absolutely no reason why an athlete with a knee injury cannot perform exercises for the entire upper torso — assuming, of course, that the exercises are done sitting or laying and not standing! Likewise, there is no reason why an athlete with a shoulder injury cannot train the muscles of the lower body.

THE LAST REP

As coaches, you have a legal responsibility to ensure the physical preparedness of your teams. In many instances, an injured area or body part can be exercised in a safe, prudent and pain-free manner. This will prevent a significant loss in muscular size and strength. And even though an athlete may not be able to exercise an injured area due to an unreasonable amount of pain or discomfort, movements can still be performed for uninjured body parts. Remember, it is very important to continue some type of strength training whenever possible — even in the event of an injury.

Chapter 6
THE IMPORTANCE OF INTENSITY

Except for genetics, an athlete's intensity of effort is arguably the most important factor in attaining the maximal possible results from strength training. Apparently, there exists a level of intensity below which little or no strength gains occur. In other words, the intensity of effort must be great enough to exceed this threshold so that a sufficient stimulus is provided for growth to take place. Failure to reach this level of intensity will result in sub-maximal gains. Unfortunately, no one knows precisely what level of intensity is necessary to stimulate muscular growth.

THE INTENSITY CONTINUUM

Even if the minimum level is unknown, we can determine the most productive level of intensity by deductive reasoning. For the moment, let's suppose that a 90% level of intensity represented the threshold for achieving maximal results. If so, how do we pinpoint 90% intensity . . . or 95% intensity . . . or any other level of intensity for that matter? Well, there are exactly two levels of intensity that can be determined rather easily. One level is 0% intensity or complete inactivity. Obviously, no intensity creates no stimulus and therefore produces no effect! The only other identifiable level happens to reside at the opposite end of the continuum, namely 100% intensity. This level of intensity is characterized by a total all-out effort for a prescribed amount of time. It is literally impossible to determine any other levels of intensity. So the only level of effort that is both productive and measurable is 100% intensity. (A level of intensity should not be confused with a percentage of maximal weight.)

TIME AND INTENSITY

The question arises: "How can I get my wrestlers to attain this level of intensity in the weight room?" There are varied opinions as to how this may be accomplished. Most suggestions center on increasing some program variable such as the number of sets, the number of exercises or the frequency of workouts. Although these may seem like valid ideas, it is very doubtful that increasing any of these will raise the intensity to a desirable level. The reason for this is simple: There is an inverse relationship between time and intensity. As the time or length of an activity increases, there is a concomitant decrease in the intensity of effort. Stated otherwise, you cannot train at a high level of intensity for long periods of time. Hey, anyone who has survived the rigors of a two-hour practice session should be able to verify this concept! By increasing sets, exercises or frequency, the training time will ultimately increase. The end result is actually a decreased level of intensity. If you understand the logic of this concept, it should now be obvious that in order to train at a high level of intensity, you must train for a relatively short period of time.

ATTAINING MAXIMAL INTENSITY

Thus far, our reasoning has established that 100% intensity is the only desirable level that we can measure. This level of intensity is best achieved when an individual trains to the point of momentary muscular fatigue. When this is attained, an athlete has stimulated the maximal number of muscle fibers for growth. How does this happen?

Let's say that one of your wrestlers is to perform a set of leg extensions with 100 pounds. In order to overcome inertia and provide impetus to the 100 pounds of resistance, his quadriceps must exert slightly more than 100 pounds of force. The weight will not move if a force less than or equal to 100 pounds is applied. During the first repetition, only a small percentage of the available muscle fibers are working — just enough to move the weight. As each repetition is performed, some muscle fibers will fatigue. Fresh fibers are simultaneously recruited to assist the fatigued fibers in generating ample force. This continues until the last repetition when momentary muscular fatigue is finally reached. At this point, the available fibers cannot produce enough force to lift the weight. During the final repetition, his level of intensity is maximal and he has stimulated as many muscle fibers as possible for growth. By performing one set with maximal effort, he has done the equivalent of a few sub-maximal sets . . . but in a shorter amount of time. So one set of an exercise performed in a high-intensity fashion is just as productive as doing multiple sets . . . and obviously more efficient in terms of time.

However, there are individuals who are cynical of this style of strength training. More often than not, it is because their response was poor. Undoubtedly, their poor response was due to sub-maximal levels of intensity. One set of an exercise can produce striking results . . . but only if that one set is a total all-out effort.

ONE MORE REP

A high level of intensity is an absolute requirement for optimal strength gains. Although it is quite possible that less than 100% intensity will provide enough of a stimulus to produce maximal results, 100% intensity is the only desirable level that can be measured. This level is typified by training to the point of muscular fatigue. By training in this manner, only one set of each prescribed exercise is required. Since it is literally impossible to train hard for long periods of time, an entire session in the weight room should not exceed about 60 minutes. At most, 17-19 total exercises should be performed per workout with the emphasis on the major muscles of the hips, legs and upper torso. Doing any more than this will probably cut into your athletes' recovery time and limit their potential gains.

Chapter 7
THE IMPORTANCE OF PROGRESSIVE OVERLOAD

In the late 1940s, the term "Progressive Resistance Exercise" was coined by Dr. Thomas L. DeLorme. In fact, he is often referred to as "the father of progressive resistance exercise." Dr. DeLorme started lifting weights in 1932 at the age of 16 in an attempt to increase his muscular size and strength. During World War II, he applied the lessons he had learned from his own experience to the rehabilitation of large numbers of wounded soldiers.

Unfortunately, little of what is done in most weight rooms can be characterized as being "progressive." It's not uncommon to hear of an athlete who performs the same number of repetitions with the same amount of weight over and over again, workout after workout. Other than not training with a high level of intensity, failing to make progressions in the weight room is probably the main reason why athletes fail to achieve their physical potential from weight training.

Suppose that today you did a set of the bench press for 10 repetitions with 200 pounds and a month later you are still doing 10 repetitions with 200 pounds. Did you increase your strength? Probably not. On the other hand, what if you were able to do 11 repetitions with 240 pounds a month later? In this case, you performed 10% more repetitions with 20% more weight — excellent progress over the course of one month.

THE OVERLOAD PRINCIPLE

One of the oldest and most often cited tenets in exercise science is known as the "Overload Principle." First dubbed in 1933, this principle states that in order for you to increase your muscular size and strength, your muscles must be stressed — or "overloaded" — with a workload that is beyond their present capacity.

Continuous employment of the Overload Principle is necessary to stimulate changes in the functional and structural abilities of your muscles. This means that your muscles must be stressed with progressively harder work if they are to continually increase in size and strength. For this reason, your muscles must experience a workload that is increased steadily and systematically throughout the course of your strength-training program — that is, with a progressive overload.

Legend has it that Milo of Crotona — an Olympic athlete in ancient Greece — periodically lifted a baby bull on his shoulders. Milo's strength increased as the bull increased in size and weight. This crude method of progressive overload was responsible for his legendary strength gains.

In modern times, a simple yet effective way to progressively overload your muscles is to incorporate the double-progressive technique. Every time you work out, you must attempt to increase either the weight you use or the repetitions you perform in relation to your previous workout. Stated otherwise, you must impose demands upon your muscles that they have not previously experienced by either using more weight or performing more repetitions than in the past. Exposing your muscles to progressively greater demands stimulates compensatory adaptation in response to the unaccustomed workload. Specifically, the adaptations are increases in muscular size and strength.

In brief, the double-progressive technique would be used in the weight room these two ways: (1) If you reach concentric muscular fatigue within your prescribed repetition range — say you did 18 repetitions and your range is 15-20 — you should repeat the weight for your next workout and try to improve upon the number of repetitions you did; and (2) If you attain or surpass the maximal number of prescribed repetitions in an exercise — say you did 16 repetitions and your range is 10-15 — you should increase the resistance for your next workout.

PROGRESSIONS: HOW MUCH?

Your progressions in resistance need not be in Herculean leaps and bounds . . . but the weight you use must always be demanding. You should increase the resistance in an amount with which you are comfortable. Fortunately, this may be accomplished much more systematically than the method used by Milo and his growing bull. Your muscles respond better if the progressions in resistance are 5% or less — depending upon the degree to which the exercise was challenging. For instance, suppose that an exercise has a repetition range of 15-20. If you barely managed to do 20 repetitions, then you should make a slightly smaller progression in resistance than if you reached muscular fatigue at 21 or 22 repetitions.

When you make smaller progressions, your muscles hardly notice the slightly heavier weight and your repetitions won't decline much if at all. In other words, it is much easier for your muscles to adapt to subtle increases in resistance than larger ones. As an example, imagine that an exercise has a repetition range of 15-20 and you did 200/20 (200 pounds/20 repetitions). If you make a 10% increase in resistance the next time you do that exercise (to 220 pounds), you will probably notice the heavier weight and it could result in a performance of 220/16. In this scenario, before you can make your next progression in resistance you must improve the number of repetitions you did by 25% (from 16 to 20) — which may prove to be a very difficult task. Conversely, if you originally increased the weight by only 2.5 pounds (to 202.5 pounds), it is not likely you will detect the slightly heavier weight and you would probably get 202.5/20. Another 2.5-pound increase the next time you do that exercise may result in 205/20. Eventually, you might progress to the point where you are doing 220/19. Compared to the previous example, it took you a few more weeks to reach 220 pounds but you allowed your body to adapt gradually. And now, you only need to increase your repetitions by one — from 19 to 20 — to make your next progression in weight.

To make slight progressions in resistance, you can use smaller "Olympic" plates on free-weight movements and plate-loaded machines. Smaller plates are made that weigh as little as 1.25 and 2.5 pounds. If lighter plates are not available, you can simply hang something from the bar (or movement arm) like a small ankle weight. Ankle weights can also be used to make progressions in dumbbell exercises. Making a progression from 20- to

25-pound dumbbells represents a 25% increase in resistance. Instead of making such a large percentage increase, you can use the 20-pound dumbbells and put 1.25-pound ankle weights around your wrists. In effect, you would be using 21.25 pounds — a more reasonable progression in weight of 6.25%.

Most selectorized machines have self-contained weight stacks with plates that usually weigh 10, 12.5, 15, 20 or 25 pounds. When using selectorized machines, you can make smaller progressions by using saddle plates — or "add-on" weights — which can be 1.25 or 2.5 pounds. (Some selectorized machines have a unique compound weight stack that enables the user to make progressions in one- or two-pound increments without having to use or search for saddle plates.) If saddle plates are not available, you can take an Olympic plate and secure it to the weight stack by first inserting a selector pin through the hole in the Olympic plate and then into one of the selectorized plates. This is often referred to as "pinning" an Olympic plate to the weight stack. You can also place any object that weighs about one or two pounds on top of a weight stack — as long as it won't fall off while you are using the equipment.

THE WORKOUT CARD

The importance of accurate record keeping cannot be overemphasized. Records are logs of what you have accomplished during each and every exercise of each and every strength session. In a sense, a workout card is a history of your activities in the weight room.

A workout card can be an extremely valuable tool to monitor your application of progressive overload. The card can take an infinite number of appearances. However, you should be able to record your bodyweight, the date of each workout, the weight used for each exercise, the number of repetitions performed for each exercise, the order in which the exercises were completed and any necessary seat adjustments.

THE BOTTOM LINE

Remember, the resistance you use must always be challenging. If you are just beginning a strength-training program or you change the exercises in your routine, it may take you several workouts before you find a challenging weight. That's okay, simply continue to make progressions in the resistance as needed.

Progressive overload has always been and will always be of utmost importance in achieving physical potential. The bottom line is that you must place a demand on your muscles that is beyond what they are accustomed. If you did 200 pounds today for 10 repetitions, then your next workout you either must attempt to do more repetitions or increase the weight. Either way, you have taken a step closer to realizing your potential as a wrestler.

Chapter 8
NEW PRESPECTIVES IN STRENGTH TRAINING

In 1986, Nautilus™ founder Arthur Jones revealed the results of a 13-year-old research project. The findings have appeared in various fitness-oriented magazines as "Exercise 1986." The project identified four physiological factors that were documented by data of incredible accuracy.

Those of us who are involved in strength training are continually bombarded by huge amounts of information. From this information, we must separate fact from fiction in order to make logical and practical applications that are in the best interests of our athletes. The implications of this breakthrough will be discussed from a coach's viewpoint and suggest how your wrestlers can correctly apply this important information in the weight room.

THE FOUR FACTORS

The four physiological factors that were revealed by Jones are as follows:

Response to Exercise

The first factor deals with an individual's response to exercise. Apparently, there exist at least two distinct types of response to exercise. These responses have been designated as Type S and Type G. Type S individuals have a specific response to exercise. Given a limited-range exercise — such as partial movements — these individuals will experience a limited-range effect. In addition, the effect is specific to the range of movement (ROM) involved in the exercise. After the initial testing of 600 subjects, it appeared that roughly 72% of a random group of people have a specific response to exercise. On the other hand, it seems that about 28% of a random sample have a general response. These individuals — Type G — obtain an effect throughout a full ROM even though exercising over a limited range.

How is this information meaningful? For years, most coaches have insisted that their athletes should exercise throughout a full ROM in order to receive a full-range effect. Does the identification of this factor mean that full-range exercise is no longer necessary? Certainly not! If anything, this factor firmly establishes the need for full-range exercise since almost three out of every four people have a specific — or Type S — response. And even if certain individuals show a general response, the results produced in the un-worked area are not in proportion to those in the worked area. Furthermore, all individuals — whether their response is specific or general — should exercise throughout a full ROM in order to maintain or promote flexibility.

This does not mean to imply that your wrestlers should avoid limited-range movements. During rehabilitation, for example, an athlete can exercise throughout a pain-free range and still manage to stimulate some gains in strength. In short, however, full-range movements are more productive and should be performed by everyone.

Magnitude of Effect

A second factor relates to the immediate — or short-term — effect of exercise. The effects of exercise vary from one individual to another. Despite training with a high level of intensity — as in achieving muscular fatigue — some individuals receive only a slight effect in that their momentary reduction in strength is quite small. Since they have made minimal inroads toward stimulating muscular growth, they receive minimal benefits. During an endurance test with 80% of their maximal strength, these individuals can perform a relatively large number of repetitions indicating a high degree of muscular endurance. Conversely, other individuals experience a great effect from high-intensity exercise. By comparison, their momentary reduction in strength is tremendous. They can perform only a few repetitions with 80% of their maximal strength.

41

This discovery does not mean that high-intensity exercise is counterproductive — although if the effect is too great, it may actually prevent muscular growth. Generally speaking, however, all individuals should train in a high-intensity fashion.

Mr. Jones' research has probably revealed a non-invasive method of determining fiber types. In all likelihood, those individuals with little effect from exercise possess a high percentage of Type I (or "slow-twitch") fibers while those who exhibit a great effect have a high percentage of Type II (or "fast-twitch") fibers.

A startling discovery? Absolutely. No longer must we ascertain fiber type by taking a plug of muscle tissue during a biopsy. More importantly, this implies that some of your wrestlers — because of their predominant fiber type — will require a slightly lower or slightly higher repetition range in order to maximize their response to exercise.

So how can wrestling coaches determine optimal repetition range for their athletes? One way is to have each wrestler perform an endurance test with 80% of his one-repetition maximum (1-RM). For example, if you have a wrestler who can do a bicep curl with 100 pounds, then 80 pounds would be used. If the athlete does a relatively high number of repetitions — more than about 15 — with 80% of his maximum, you can assume his biceps are primarily composed of slow-twitch (ST) fibers and, in this case, increase his repetition range to about 12-15. On the other hand, if he performed a rather low number of repetitions — less than 5 or 6 — with 80% of his 1-RM, it is likely that his biceps are mostly composed of fast-twitch (FT) fibers and, in this case, his training response will be greater from a lower repetition range of about 6-9. Since the distribution of fiber types varies from muscle to muscle, an endurance test would have to be performed for each muscle group.

Unfortunately, determining an athlete's 1-RM for most exercises is somewhat dangerous when using conventional equipment and, therefore, not recommended. However, a less accurate — albeit much safer — means of estimating individual repetition ranges can be used. Suppose an athlete reaches muscular fatigue on the leg extension using 100 pounds and a training partner immediately reduces the weight by 25-30% (to 70-75 pounds) after the final repetition. If the lifter performs a good deal more than 3-4 repetitions with 70-75 pounds, his momentary reduction in strength was low. This would suggest that his quadriceps probably have a relatively high percentage of ST fibers. If the lifter does fewer than 3-4 repetitions with 70-75 pounds, his reduction in strength was high. This would suggest that his quadriceps probably have a relatively high percentage of FT fibers. Again, this procedure is not nearly as precise as doing an endurance test but it is intriguing and somewhat safer.

It should also be noted that previously suggested repetition ranges — that is, 15-20 for the hips, 10-15 for the legs and 6-12 for the upper body — still serve as excellent guidelines for the majority of people. Although, it now appears that we can accelerate some individuals' responses to exercise by modifying those ranges slightly.

Recovery Ability

The next factor pertains to an area of major concern for wrestling coaches: recovery ability. It seems that some individuals have a rather high tolerance for exercise and recover quickly; others have a low tolerance for exercise and recover somewhat slowly. An individual who has poor recovery ability must train cautiously in order to avoid poor results.

Most individuals require about 48-72 hours of recovery time between strength workouts. As a coach, you can identify those wrestlers who have a low tolerance for exercise simply by monitoring their progress in the weight room. Athletes who fail to show progress over the course of a few workouts may need additional recovery time.

Remember, an athlete need only perform one set of each exercise to the point of momentary muscular fatigue to achieve maximal gains. An entire routine should consist of no more than about 17-19 exercises. The addition of either more sets or more exercises will only increase the probability that the demands will exceed the athlete's recovery ability and result in a loss of strength. If anything, the volume of work done in the weight room should be reduced when progress reaches a plateau.

Incidentally, lack of progress during the wresting season is not unusual. Because of the increased activity level, gains in the weight room may be minimal at best. For this reason, your athletes should strength train no more than twice a week during the season to allow for adequate recovery.

The Strength Ratio

The final factor deals with the relationship between three distinct levels of strength: concentric, isometric and eccentric. Your concentric (or positive) and eccentric (or negative) levels of strength represent your ability to raise and lower a weight, respectively; your isometric (or static) level of strength relates to your ability to hold a weight in one position. You can hold statically about 20% more than you can raise; you can lower eccentrically about 40% more than you can raise. So, if you can lift 100 pounds, you can hold statically about 120 pounds and you can lower eccentrically about 140 pounds. The difference in strength is possibly due to the effects of internal muscular friction.

This so-called "strength ratio" has been established for fresh muscles. Furthermore, it is a relatively constant ratio. In other words, if you increase the eccentric strength of a muscle, both your concentric and isometric strength will increase accordingly. But again, this ratio is only true of fresh muscles. As a muscle tires, the ratio of strength changes dramatically. When your concentric strength has fatigued to the point that you can no longer raise a weight, your reserve of eccentric strength is still enormous. In fact, your eccentric strength may be as much as 50 times greater than your concentric strength in extreme cases of muscular fatigue.

As Mr. Jones points out, this factor can be extremely important during the rehabilitation of injuries. For example, if a wrestler with a severely atrophied limb — such as might be found when a cast is removed — does not have the strength to raise even the lightest of weights, he may be able to lower the weight. In this way, the muscle can still be stimulated to grow and get stronger. And remember that an increase in eccentric strength

44

will produce an increase in concentric strength.

The practical application of this factor in the weight room is quite similar. Suppose that a chin bar is the only piece of equipment that is available to train your upper-back musculature. Let's also assume that your heavyweight does not possess adequate upper-body strength to pull his chest to the bar. Instead of neglecting this exercise altogether, he can perform the movement in a "negative-only" manner. This is done by starting the exercise in the contracted position with his chest touching the bar and then lowering himself to the stretched position in about 6-8 seconds. One set of this exercise done in a negative-only manner to the point of muscular fatigue will stimulate his musculature to increase in size and strength. Athletes may also perform this and other movements in a "negative-only" manner in order to provide for variety in their training. The previously stated guidelines for the negative-only chin apply to other exercises as well except that the weight that is used initially should be at least 10% more than could normally be handled in a traditional fashion. (Keep in mind, too, that — other than dips and chins — negative-only exercise requires the use of one or more training partners to help do the concentric portion of the repetition.)

This factor also seems to suggest that greater gains can be produced when a few post-fatigue "negative" repetitions are performed immediately following muscular fatigue. When a lifter reaches muscular fatigue, it is because the concentric strength has become exhausted such that the weight simply cannot be raised. Again, the eccentric strength is still very high. Therefore, a training partner (or coach) can assist the lifter in raising the weight while the lifter resists the movement during the lowering phase. Post-fatigue repetitions will cause a greater reduction in an individual's momentary strength thereby causing a greater effect (provided that the reduction in strength is not too great). The end result is a more efficient and more productive method of training.

Finally, since individuals can lower more weight than they can raise, it stands to reason that the eccentric phase of the movement should be emphasized. In other words, if you raise a weight in 1-2 seconds, you should lower it in about 3-4 seconds. Indeed, the eccentric phase of a repetition is at least as important as the concentric phase.

CONCLUDING REMARKS

At this point in time it may seem somewhat premature to describe Mr. Jones' research as the most significant findings ever made in the field of exercise. However, the potential far-reaching effects of these four physiological factors are staggering. Understanding these factors and properly applying them to your strength program could very well mean the difference between average results and superior ones.

Chapter 9

TEN MYTHS IN STRENGTH AND FITNESS

Perhaps no other discipline is ripe with more myths than strength and fitness. What follows are ten of the more popular myths.

Myth 1: *Free weights are better than machines for improving muscular strength.* In order for wrestlers to increase their strength, an adequate load (or resistance) must be applied to their muscles and the workload must be progressively more challenging. Muscles can be "loaded" using a variety of equipment including barbells, dumbbells, machines (selectorized or plate-loaded), cinder blocks, other wrestlers (when doing manual-resistance exercises) or a wrestler's own bodyweight (when doing dips and chins). A wrestler's response to strength training is primarily a function of individual genetics and their level of intensity (or effort)   not the equipment that is used.

Myth 2: *In order to become more explosive on the mat, wrestlers must lift explosively in the weight room.* There is no scientific evidence to suggest that performing repetitions with rapid speeds of movement will make wrestlers more explosive on the wrestling mat. When repetitions are performed explosively, there is a load on the muscles in the first part of the movement but not on the last part of the movement. More importantly, the faster a weight is lifted the more dangerous it becomes. Therefore, repetitions should be performed with a deliberate, controlled speed of movement to make the exercise more efficient and reduce the risk of injury.

Myth 3: *Wrestlers need to consume large amounts of protein.* Some research suggests that active individuals need more protein than the established Recommended Dietary Allowance (RDA) of 0.8

grams per kilogram of bodyweight per day. But, these greater protein requirements are usually met quite easily through a normal intake of foods. However, wrestlers who are vegetarians may require protein supplementation to meet their daily needs.

Myth 4: A high-volume approach is the key to maximizing strength. A "More-is-Better" attitude is not necessarily better when it comes to strength training. If a greater volume of strength training was the key, then two sets would be better than one set, three sets would be better than two sets which are better than one set, four sets would be better than three sets which are better than two sets which are better than one set and so on. If anything, the key to maximizing strength is the level of intensity in the weight room. Remember, too, that as the level of intensity increases, the volume of activity must decrease. Therefore, if a strength-training workout is to be intense, it simply cannot involve a high volume of activity.

Myth 5: Power cleans are specific to many wrestling skills. The word "specific" means "exact" or "identical," not "similar" or "just like." The only skill that is identical to a power clean is a power clean. Whenever a wrestling skill is performed, it involves a certain neuromuscular pattern that is unique to the skill. Simulating the skill with a weighted object — such as a barbell — involves a totally different neuromuscular program. At best, trying to imitate wrestling skills with weighted objects is a waste of time; at worst, it creates neuromuscular confusion such that the previously established skill patterns must be relearned. The best way for athletes to improve a wrestling skill is to practice the exact skill over and over and over again until it is instinctive. Furthermore, the skill must be practiced with perfect technique exactly as it would be done in a match. There is no exercise done in the weight room — with barbells or machines — that is specific to any wrestling skill.

Myth 6: Split routines are better than total-body workouts. From an athletic perspective, split routines are not recommended because they are not specific to the muscular involvement of wrestling. When you use a split routine, you exercise different muscles on different days. However, a selective use of muscles never happens in a wrestling match. In a match, wrestlers are required to integrate all of their muscle groups at once. Therefore, it makes little sense for wrestlers to prepare for competition by training their muscles separately on different days.

Myth 7: Periodization is the best method for increasing strength. Periodization is the preferred training method of competitive weightlifters who must "peak" for a one-repetition maximum. For the most part, competitive weightlifters must "peak" for only two or three contests a year. On the other hand, wrestlers have to "peak" for dozens of matches a year — sometimes several in one day. In addition, periodization is characterized by pre-planned workouts that can be unnecessarily complicated and do not take into account individual differences in trainability. Besides, there is an abundance of scientific and anecdotal evidence pointing to the fact that many different methods can increase muscular strength.

Myth 8: Wrestlers who lift weights to the point of muscular failure are teaching themselves to fail. Since training to muscular failure (or fatigue) is essentially using a high degree of effort and training to exhaustion, this would also mean that anytime wrestlers pushed themselves to exhaustion — whether it be at a practice or match or conditioning run or anything else — they were teaching themselves to fail. This makes no sense whatsoever. If anything, wrestlers who stop short of muscular failure are teaching themselves to give up. In order to ensure maximal results from strength training, it is necessary to lift weights with a high level of intensity — which is characterized by lifting to the point of muscular failure.

Myth 9: High-Intensity Training (HIT) is "one set of 8-12 repetitions on Nautilus™ machines." Even if this statement were true, it would still be a gross oversimplification of HIT. In fact, one of the great attributes of HIT is its versatility. First of all, HIT does not have to be one set of an exercise — it is not uncommon for HIT practioners to recommend two or three sets of an exercise. Repetition ranges can also be manipulated to provide variety in training and to reduce the orthopedic stress in younger wrestlers or for the purposes of rehabilitation. Moreover, the resistance used in HIT can come from any type of equipment or "tool." Incidentally, the speed of movement, volume of work-outs, sequence of exercises, duration of workouts and frequency of training can all be varied as well.

Myth 10: *Princeton University does not have a wrestling team.* This has absolutely nothing to do with strength and fitness, but it is a myth nonetheless! In recent years, the wrestling program has gone through turbulent times. However, the program remains intact. In fact, Princeton University has competed in the Eastern Intercollegiate Wrestling Association (EIWA) tournament every year since 1906, having won the very first championship. In addition, the National Wrestling Coaches Association named Princeton University the 1996 Academic National Champions. Head Coach Michael New also served as the secretary for the Ivy League Wrestling Coaches Association. Finally, Princeton University was the host school for the first-ever Ivy League Wrestling Championships on November 15, 1997. Recruiting efforts and a dedicated base of talent assure that the program will be competitive again in the not too distant future. [Note: Princeton University qualified three wrestlers for the 2001 NCAA Championships.]

Chapter 10

COACH, I WANNA BE EXPLOSIVE!

I wish I had a buck for every time I have heard athletes make that statement. Indeed, athletes (and coaches) are always looking for ways to increase speed, power and explosiveness. The search for these valuable athletic components has led to one of the most hotly debated subjects in strength training. The debate concerns the speed at which an exercise or movement should be performed. Essentially, there are two schools of thought: Some strength and fitness professionals advocate high velocity/explosive movements that are ballistic in nature, whereas others recommend deliberate movements that are performed in a controlled manner.

FIBER RECRUITMENT

Most of the controversy pertains to the recruitment of muscle fibers. Proponents of high-velocity movements argue that in order to become "explosive," you must train "explosive." Their assumption is that by lifting explosively in the weight room, the fast speed of movement will somehow change the chemical composition of the slow-twitch (ST) fibers and/or preferentially recruit the fast-twitch (FT) fibers.

Well, that sounds great except for the fact that there is no conclusive evidence in the literature to firmly establish the belief that muscle fibers can be changed from one type to another. It is also important to note that muscle fibers are recruited in an orderly fashion according to the intensity or force requirements and not by the speed of movement. Demands of low muscular intensity are met by the ST fibers. Intermediate fibers are recruited once the ST fibers are no longer able to continue the task. The FT fibers are finally recruited only when the other fibers cannot meet the force requirements. All fibers are working when the FT fibers are being used. In short, there is absolutely no definitive evidence in the literature to imply that movements performed in an explosive or ballistic manner will bypass the ST and intermediate fibers in order to specifically recruit the FT fibers.

MOMENTUM

Besides the fact that high-velocity movements do not selectively recruit the FT fibers or alter the composition of the ST fibers, this method of training is not recommended for reasons that are much more serious. Lifting a weight at a rapid speed of movement increases the involvement of momentum. After the initial explosive movement, the muscles gradually become "unloaded" throughout the remaining range of motion. In simple terms, the weight is practically moving under its own power.

To illustrate the effects of momentum on muscular tension, imagine that you pushed a 100-pound cart a distance of 50 yards at a deliberate, steady pace. In this instance, you maintained a constant tension on your muscles for the entire 50 yards. Now, suppose that you were to push the same cart another 50 yards. This time, however, you accelerated your pace to the point where you were running as fast as possible. If you were to stop pushing the cart after 35 yards, the cart would continue to move by itself because momentum became excessive. So your muscles were loaded during the first 35 yards . . . but not during the final 15 yards. The same effect occurs in the weight room. When weights are lifted explosively, the muscles are loaded briefly during the initial part of the movement . . . but not during the last part. In effect, the requirement for muscular force is lessened and the potential strength gains are reduced accordingly.

More importantly, using an excessive amount of momentum to lift a weight increases the internal forces encountered by a given joint; the faster a weight is lifted, the greater these forces are amplified. These high forces are created at the point of explosion. When the forces exceed the structural limits of a joint, an injury occurs in the muscles, bones or connective tissue. Quick question: Do you know what the exact tensile strength of ligaments and tendons is at any given moment? Well, I sure do not — and neither does anyone else. In fact, the only way we can ascertain tensile strength is when the structural limits are surpassed. Then, of course, it is too late. Therefore, we must be concerned with an exercise's speed of movement because we simply do not know the structural limitations of the various connective tissues in the human body.

The potentially damaging effects of high-speed movements can be demonstrated rather easily using an ordinary 16-ounce hammer. Suppose you were to take the hammer and lay it across your hand. It is doubtful that this action would elicit any feelings of pain or discomfort. Next, imagine that you lifted the hammer and allowed it to drop on your hand from a height of about a foot. There is no doubt that this action would tend to hurt a bit. But why would dropping a hammer on your hand cause significantly more pain (and damage) than resting it on your hand? After all, in both cases the weight of the hammer remains unchanged. The answer has to do with velocity. A hammer resting on your hand has a velocity of zero; by dropping the same hammer, you would increase its velocity and, in effect, magnify its force.

Assuming that an object's mass (or weight) does not change, the amount of potential force is then directly related to the object's acceleration. In other words, as the speed of movement increases, so does its potential force. This is not merely my opinion or observation — it is a fundamental law of physics. Something new? Nope. In fact, it was first proposed about 300 years ago by a fellow named Isaac Newton and is referred to as his "Second Law of Motion."

The potentially destructive forces created by high-velocity movements are violently illustrated every minute on our nation's highways. Literally. Of course, not all automobile accidents can be attributed to high speeds of movement. However, it is true that a slower velocity would certainly lessen the risk and potential for injury . . . not to mention the severity. And if slower speeds of movement are safer, doesn't it follow that faster speeds of movement are more dangerous?

Proponents of explosive training sometimes counter these facts by saying, "So what? Sports are dangerous — just look at football and wrestling. Maybe we should stop playing sports." Arguments like this miss the point entirely. It is true that sports are inherently dangerous. However, that does not justify using potentially dangerous techniques in the weight room in search of "explosiveness." Indeed, encouraging anyone to explode with a weight is suggesting musculoskeletal trauma. The only thing that might explode is your biological tissue from its point of insertion.

Dr. Fred Allman — a past president of the American College of Sports Medicine — takes this point one step further, stating, "It is even possible that many injuries . . . may be the result of weakened connective tissue caused by explosive training in the weight room."

A SAFER WAY

It is rather obvious that explosive movements are unproductive and potentially destructive. Anyone who does not believe that an injury can occur from a ballistic movement has apparently never heard of whiplash.

Absolutely no one knows exactly how fast an exercise should be performed, nor do I think that anyone will ever know. It must certainly differ from one individual to another and probably even varies within the same person from one week to the next depending upon that person's current level of strength and conditioning. At any rate, one thing is certain: It is much safer and more efficient to lift weights under control. Athletes should be required to raise the weight without any jerking or explosive movements and to lower it under control. Raising the weight in about 1-2 seconds and lowering it in about 3-4 seconds will ensure that speeds of movement are not ballistic in nature and that momentum does not play a significant role in the efficiency of the exercise.

IMPROVING EXPLOSIVENESS

When someone is described as being "explosive" on an athletic field, essentially what we are saying is that the athlete performs, moves or reacts quickly and forcefully. This is primarily due to the fact that the athlete's movement patterns for a particular skill are so firmly ingrained in his "motor memory" that there is little or no wasted effort. In other words, the athlete is highly efficient at performing the intended sports skill.

In order for you (or your wrestlers) to become more explosive, there are two things that you must do. First of all, you must literally practice the motor skills for thousands and thousands of task-specific repetitions. Each repetition must be done with perfect technique so that its specific movement pattern becomes firmly established in your motor memory. It is important to remember that the skill must be practiced perfectly and exactly as you would use it in competition. Remember, practice makes perfect . . . but only if you practice perfect.

Secondly, you must strengthen the major muscle groups that are used during the performance of that skill. However, this should not be done in a manner that attempts to mimic a particular skill so as not to confuse or inhibit the intended movement pattern. A stronger muscle can produce more force; if you can produce more force, you will require less effort and be able to perform the skill more quickly, more efficiently and more explosively. But again, this is provided that you have practiced enough in a correct manner so that you will be more skillful in applying that force. So if your goal is to become more explosive, you must become proficient at your wrestling techniques and you must strengthen the muscles of your hips, legs and upper torso.

Chapter 11

ADOLESCENT STRENGTH TRAINING

Years ago, the literature contained very little useful information concerning the needs of the adolescent athlete. At that time, strength training had not really been accepted or emphasized during the younger ages. This was unfortunate, since younger athletes have a great deal to gain from weight training. Nowadays, there is much more information available on this topic and adolescents are no strangers to the weight room.

A safe, practical and productive strength program can prepare adolescents for the demands of sport. Strengthening their muscles, joints and connective tissue is an excellent precautionary measure against injury. In addition, they can perform closer to their potential by increasing their functional strength.

What's the earliest age that an individual can initiate strength training? There is no clear-cut borderline for determining a safe age at which to begin strength training because each person "ages" at a different rate. However, most youths are physically mature enough to begin strength training at about the age of 13 or 14.

GENERAL GUIDELINES

With some modifications, virtually all of the strength-training guidelines that I have suggested in the past for athletes can also apply to adolescents. The modified guidelines are as follows:

Intensity

Anyone who has read my writings knows that I advocate a strength program that is performed in a high-intensity fashion. For those of you who are unfamiliar with "high-intensity training," it is characterized by performing each exercise to the point of muscular fatigue.

Younger teens may not be comfortable training to the point of muscular fatigue. Hey, this might be too demanding for some of your older athletes! Youths who are not comfortable with this level of intensity can terminate the exercise a few repetitions short of muscular fatigue. There is nothing wrong with that. As the teen develops physically, the intensity can be gradually increased.

Older and physically mature teens can increase the intensity of the exercise by performing 3-4 additional post-fatigue repetitions after reaching muscular fatigue. The two most popular types of post-fatigue repetitions are negatives and breakdowns. These intensification repetitions will allow the muscles to be overloaded in a safe, efficient manner. (It should be noted that post-fatigue repetitions should be used carefully and infrequently and only with physically mature teens.)

Repetitions

Many adolescents will want to "max out" to see how much they can lift for one repetition. Never — and I mean NEVER — have them max out. Seeing how much weight they can lift should not be viewed as a "right of passage" into adulthood. Maxing out substantially increases their risk of injury and proves absolutely nothing. Remember, the winner of a wrestling match has never been decided by a bench-press contest.

In fact, younger and physically immature teens should use slightly higher repetition ranges — such as 20-25 repetitions for exercises involving their hips, 15-20 repetitions for their legs and 10-15 repetitions for their upper torso. The higher repetition ranges will necessitate using somewhat lighter weights, which will in turn reduce the stress placed upon their bones and joints.

Older and physically mature teens should reach muscular fatigue within 15-20 repetitions for exercises involving their hips, 10-15 repetitions for their legs and 6-12 repetitions for their upper torso.

If muscular fatigue occurs before the lower level of the repetition range is reached, the weight is too heavy and should be reduced for the next workout. If the upper level of the repetition range is exceeded before muscular fatigue is experienced, the weight is too light and should be increased for the next workout by about 5% or less.

Technique

Adolescents should be required to perform their repetitions in a deliberate, controlled manner without any jerking movements. Raising a weight in a rapid, explosive fashion is ill-advised for two reasons: (1) it introduces an excessive amount of momentum into the movement which makes the exercise less productive and less efficient and (2) it exposes the muscles, joint structures and connective tissue to potentially dangerous forces which magnify the likelihood of incurring an injury while strength training. Raising a weight in about 1-2 seconds guarantees that an adolescent is exercising in a safe, efficient manner.

Also, everyone — especially younger athletes — should perform each exercise throughout the greatest possible range of motion that safety allows. This will promote or maintain flexibility.

Duration

A productive workout for younger and physically immature teens can be performed in about 20-30 minutes. Older and physically mature teens should limit their workout to about 60 minutes or less. Youths do not need to spend much more time than that engaged in strength-training activities. The risk of overuse injuries will be greatly reduced by eliminating marathon strength sessions in the weight room.

Volume

For younger and physically immature teens, a workout should consist of about 12 exercises or less. Older and physically mature teens should do no more than about 17-19 exercises during each workout. This lower volume of exercises decreases the potential for overuse injury.

Younger and physically immature teens should perform one exercise for their hips, hamstrings, quadriceps, calves/dorsi flexors, chest, upper back, shoulders, lower arms, abdominals and lower back. Two exercises should be done for their necks to strengthen and protect their cervical areas against possible traumatic injury. For older and physically mature teens, one exercise should be performed for their hips, hamstrings, quadriceps, calves/dorsi flexors, biceps, triceps, lower arms, abdominals and lower back. Two exercises should be selected for their chest, upper back (the "lats") and shoulders. They should also include 2-4 exercises for their necks. Youths should select any exercises they prefer in order to train those body parts, provided that the exercises they choose can be done safely.

The fact of the matter is that more is not necessarily better when it comes to strength training. Performing too many exercises may produce too much muscular fatigue which will not permit muscular growth — and may even produce a loss in muscular size and strength. In addition, the more exercises that are performed, the harder it will be to maintain a desirable level of intensity. Remember, a large amount of low-intensity exercise will do very little in the way of increasing strength.

Occasionally, an extra movement may be performed to emphasize a particular body part. However, if a youth starts to level off or "plateau" in one or more exercises, it's probably from doing too many movements.

In terms of exercise selection, movements that involve the bodyweight as resistance — such as the dip, chin, push-up and sit-up — along with partner- or manual-resisted movements are extremely productive for building strength. In particular, dips and chins work every major muscle in the upper torso.

Frequency

To lessen the risk of overuse injury, younger and physically immature teens should strength train 1-2 times per week. As the teen matures physically, strength training can be increased to 2-3 days per week. Strength training places great demands and stress on the muscles. Performing any more than three sessions a week will gradually become counterproductive if the demands placed on the muscles exceed their recovery ability.

Athletes are encouraged to continue strength training even while in-season or while competing to maintain (or improve) their strength throughout the wrestling season. However, the frequency of workouts should be reduced due to the increased activity level of practices and competitions. If two weekly work-outs are performed, one session should be done as soon as possible following a competition and another performed 48 hours or more before the next competition. So youths who compete on Saturdays and Tuesdays should strength train on Sundays and Wednesdays (or Thursdays — providing that it is not within 48 hours of the next competition). From time to time, a youth may only be able to strength train once a week because of a particularly heavy schedule such as competing three times in one week.

ONE MORE REP

I encourage all wrestling coaches to initiate a strength-training program for their younger athletes. In addition to being an injury-prevention mechanism, weight training is an excellent way of instilling a favorable work ethic at an early age. Make sure your young wrestlers realize the value of dedication, discipline and hard work as a way of achieving athletic ambitions.

One final note concerns a study out of Penn State that sought to determine the extent of steroid usage at the high-school level. The results of this particular research study suggested that 250,000-500,000 adolescents are using or have used steroids! Frankly, I am simply stunned by such staggering numbers. Moreover, the study also revealed that some individuals obtained the drugs from doctors, pharmacists and — believe it or not — veterinarians! (I would not be surprised to learn that some drugs had been supplied by overzealous coaches.)

The dangerous side effects from steroid use are well documented. Briefly, steroids have been linked to extreme mood swings (which can be borderline psychotic), severe acne, baldness, temporary sterility, abnormal liver function, high blood pressure, cardiovascular disease and possibly cancer of the liver and testicles. Steroids are bad news! In addition to being harmful, non-prescription steroids are illegal as well as unethical for use as performance enhancers. Instruct your athletes to steer clear of all drugs — not just steroids. Remember, users are losers. You do not need drugs to be a winner.

Chapter 12
THE TRAP BAR:
A PRODUCTIVE ALTERNATIVE

What in blazes is a trap bar? Well, a trap bar has an open, diamond-shaped center that allows the lifter to perform exercises from within the bar's opening. In a sense, the lifter is inside the bar.

EXERCISES

As the name suggests, the trap bar is primarily used to exercise the trapezius or "traps." However, there are other muscle groups that can be exercised with this piece of equipment as well.

Shrugs

A shoulder shrug is the best exercise for isolating the trapezius. I have been training my traps with shrugs on a regular basis for years — sometimes using dumbbells and other times using the bench-press station of a Universal Multi-Gym. I usually make it a practice not to write or talk about specific weights and repetitions that I use when I train but in this case, it is important here to make a later comparison. At a bodyweight of about 175 pounds, I have done shrugs with 100-pound dumbbells for as many as 17 repetitions and with 315 pounds on the Universal Multi-Gym for 9 repetitions. I really do not like to do shrugs with a barbell for several reasons. First of all, the bar rubs against my upper thighs creating additional friction and discomfort. Secondly, holding the bar in front of my body and pulling with "round shoulders" feels awkward. Finally, the angle of pull does not seem desirable for hitting my traps the right way. I feel that shrugging with the weight at my sides — as when using dumbbells or a Universal Multi-Gym — makes the movement infinitely more comfortable and gives me a much better angle of pull that is more effective for exercising my traps. However, after many years of doing shrugs this way it was time for a change. I was bored with performing them on the Universal Multi-Gym and dumbbells over 100 pounds are usually hard to find. Recently, I got to use a trap bar for the first time. Since I had never used the bar before, I was not sure of how much weight to use. After a little trial and error, I ended up doing 15 repetitions-to-fatigue with 135 pounds. Yet, despite this seemingly light weight, I woke up the next morning and every square inch of my traps was extremely sore — from the base of my skull across to my rear deltoids and all the way down to my seventh lumbar! Hey, I would have to say that the trap bar passed the litmus test. It is an excellent tool for training the trapezius in a safe, productive and comfortable manner.

Squats

Those who know my opinion about barbell squats are usually quite surprised to learn that I actually used to do that particular movement all the time. In fact, I had competed for several years as a powerlifter in the United States Marine Corps and later for the Penn State powerlifting team. At a sanctioned powerlifting meet in 1982, I managed to squat 410 pounds (and deadlift 440) at a bodyweight of 162. That may not sound like a lot of weight but consider the fact that I was at a distinct biomechanical disadvantage for the sport: I was almost 5'11" tall! Anybody who knows anything about powerlifting will tell you that the best squatters generally have short legs, a short torso, wide hips and a thick mid-section. Needless to say, I was not your prototypical squatter.

On May 10, 1983, I decided to stop doing barbell squats. The main reason was that after years of squatting (and deadlifting) with heavy weights for low repetitions, my right hip flexor was so inflamed that I could not even squat 135 pounds without experiencing a searing pain in my frontal hip area. My knees and lower back did not feel too well, either. Not to change the subject, but knee wraps do not really protect the knees. Knee wraps are used to create an artificial rebound effect out of the bottom position of the squat — similar to compressing a spring — to enable someone to lift more weight. Anyway, my buddies used to laugh at me because my knees made the same sounds as when you pour milk on Rice Krispies. I was 25 years old. (To this day, my knees still go "snap crackle pop" and I cannot stay in a crouched position for more than a few seconds because of the pain.) I also did not like the idea that after a competition, my lumbar area was literally black and blue for days and so stiff that I could not even bend over to tie my shoelaces. There are those who claim that the barbell squat is the be-all and end-all in lifting and that anybody who does not squat is basically a geek. Well, the fact is that barbell squats compress the spinal column and create excessive shearing forces in the knee joint. Anyone who does not believe that should take a class in physics or read a good biomechanics book. Sure, there are a few wide-bodied mesomorphs who can do barbell squats in a relatively safe fashion but most of us regular types have no business doing barbell squats. Period. Except for a few times when I demonstrated proper technique for a beginner powerlifter, over the last ten years I can remember squatting with a barbell exactly twice. In both instances, I just wanted to see how it felt to squat with a barbell again. My joints remembered very quickly.

Since 1983, I have been training my hips mostly with various leg presses (both selectorized and plate-loaded), a hip-and-back machine, a hip-abduction machine and a safe-squat machine. Incidentally, the safe squat is a highly innovative machine in which a person squats with the weightload on the hips — not the shoulders — which essentially eliminates spinal compression. A person can also position the lower leg so that it is roughly perpendicular to the ground thereby reducing the shear forces in the knee joint. With no exception, training to fatigue with the safe squat is the nastiest, most demanding exercise I have ever done in my life. And I have done plenty of nasty, demanding exercises in my life. It is downright brutal. After one set-to-fatigue followed by a few additional forced repetitions with the help of a training partner, my hips would throb so badly that I thought they were going to burst through my shorts. Not only that, but I was huffing and puffing like I just ran a half mile with a proverbial piano on my back. It is one tough exercise but very few facilities have one because . . . well, because it is one tough exercise!

But get this: If you place the trap bar on the floor and stand inside the opening, you can perform deadlifts/hack squats. With the weights at your sides, it is a lot easier to do the movement with proper technique, the bar does not rub up and down your body and there is no weight on your shoulders to smoosh your vertebrae together. Indeed, the trap bar provides a safe, productive alternative to the barbell squat.

Seated Press

The third movement that can be done with the trap bar is a seated press. The unique design of the bar enables you to perform this movement with a parallel grip that is similar to that used with dumbbells. You will need two spotters to give you the bar, however. Some people find that this particular grip — that is, with your palms facing each other — is more comfortable and does not "pinch" the shoulders like a behind-the-neck seated press.

OVERTIME

You are limited in the number of exercises that you can do with the trap bar. Still, the few exercises that can be performed with this bar are as effective and productive as those done with a standard Olympic bar while providing a higher level of safety and comfort. Truly, the trap bar supplies a productive alternative to several traditional exercises.

Chapter 13
STRENGTHENING THE ABDOMINALS

The importance of strengthening the abdominals or "abs" cannot be overemphasized. The functions of the mid-section include flexion, lateral flexion and rotation of the torso as well as flexion of the hip. Collectively, the muscles of this region keep the abdominal organs compressed and assist in forced expiration such as during vigorous exercise. Therefore, virtually all sports require the use of the abdominals to some degree.

BASIC ANATOMY AND MUSCULAR FUNCTION

The abdominal muscles can be divided into two basic groups: the "upper" and the "lower." (Although, technically, there is no such thing as "upper" and "lower" abdominals, these designations refer to their general anatomical locations.)

Upper Abdominals

The upper abdominal wall consists of four pairs of thin muscles arranged in layers connecting the rib cage with the pelvic girdle. The muscle fibers run in three different directions: diagonally, vertically and horizontally. This myological arrangement helps to strengthen the abdominal wall and to stabilize the trunk.

The external obliques are the outermost covering of the three layers on both sides of the abdomen. The fibers of this broad muscle form a "\ /" across the front of the abdominal area, extending diagonally downward from the lower ribs to the pubic bone. The function of the external obliques is lateral flexion to the same side and rotation of the torso to the opposite side.

The internal obliques lie immediately under the external obliques on both sides of the abdomen. These fibers form a

"/\" (an inverted "\/") along the front of the abdominal wall, extending diagonally upward from the pubic bone to the ribs. The function of the internal obliques is lateral flexion to the same side and rotation of the torso to the same side.

The rectus abdominis lies on the same layer as the internal obliques. It is a long, narrow muscle that runs vertically across the front of the abdomen from the rib cage to the pubic bone. The fibers of this muscle are interrupted along their course by three horizontal fibrous bands which give rise to the phrase "washboard abs" when describing an especially well-developed abdomen. The rectus abdominis flexes the torso toward the lower body.

The transverse abdominis is the innermost layer of the abdominal wall. It is the thinnest of all abdominal muscles and its fibers run horizontally across the abdomen. The primary function of this muscle is to constrict the abdomen such as during respiration.

Lower Abdominals

The lower abdominal muscles are primarily the iliacus and the psoas major which are located on the front hip area. These two muscles are often jointly referred to as the "iliopsoas," since they have a common tendon of insertion. The main function of the iliopsoas is to flex the hip (bring the knees to the chest).

GENERAL GUIDELINES

The following general guidelines apply when training the abdominals:

1. Exercise the abs at the end of your workout. Remember, the abdominals stabilize the rib cage and aid in forced expiration. So it would not be wise to fatigue your midsection early in your workout since this would detract from your performance in the other exercises that involve the larger, more powerful muscles — that is, your hips, legs and upper torso.

2. Exercise the upper abs before the lower abs. When performing a conventional sit-up, for example, a person uses the rectus abdominis and iliopsoas (or hip flexor). The

iliopsoas is the "weak link" in executing a sit-up. This means that your hip flexors — that is, your lower abs — will fatigue well before your upper abs. Therefore, it would be a mistake to pre-fatigue the hip flexors first because you would then weaken an already weak link thereby limiting the effect of the exercise on the upper abdominals.

3. Perform all exercises in good form. Good form is raising the weight without using a significant amount of momentum in about 1-2 seconds, pausing distinctly in the contracted (or mid-range) position and lowering the weight under control in about 3-4 seconds. This will ensure that most of the work is being done by your abdominal muscles — rather than momentum — and that your chances of incurring an injury while strength training are minimized.

4. Avoid hyperextending the spine. People frequently complain of low-back pain while executing abdominal exercises. This is usually the result of having relatively weak lumbar extensors, performing the exercise incorrectly or a combination of the two. For instance, the sit-up — or any variation of a sit-up — should be performed with your knees bent and your chin tucked into your chest. This will help keep your lower back flat, thereby reducing the amount of stress placed on it during the performance of the exercise. Under no circumstances should the so-called "Roman Chair" sit-up be done because this particular movement hyperextends the spine and places unnecessary stress on the low-back area. In the case of weak low-back muscles, strengthening exercises — such as the back extensions — should be prescribed.

5. Keep the abdominals loaded for the entire duration of the exercise. As an example, your abdominals are used during the first 30 degrees of a conventional bent-knee sit-up movement (with respect to the horizontal). So it is not necessary to raise your torso all the way to your legs. In fact, when performing a bent-knee sit-up, you should

stop before your upper torso goes beyond a point that is perpendicular to the ground. In addition, do not let your head touch the floor (or sit-up bench/board, if used) between repetitions. Otherwise, you will unload your abdominals, allowing them to rest and momentarily recover.

6. Reach momentary muscular fatigue between 8-12 repetitions (or about 50-70 seconds). Momentary muscular fatigue may best be defined as that instant when it is literally impossible for you to perform another repetition in good form. It is not necessary to perform thousands — or even hundreds — of repetitions in order to strengthen the abdominals. The abdominals should be treated like any other muscle group. Once an activity for the abdominals exceeds about 70 seconds in duration, it becomes an increasingly greater test of aerobic endurance rather than muscular strength. (It has been noted elsewhere that upper-body exercises should be performed for about 6-12 repetitions, assuming a 6-second repetition. Exercises for the abdominals have relatively short ranges of motion and require a minor adjustment in the minimum number of repetitions to ensure that the muscles are loaded for an adequate amount of time. Thus, the abdominal exercises should be done for 8-12 repetitions to guarantee a desirable amount of contraction time.)

EXERCISES

The following is a specific description of various abdominal exercises that can be performed using conventional equipment:

Sit-Up

Perhaps the most traditional movement for exercising the abdominals is the sit-up (which is often done on a bench or board). Unfortunately, this exercise is usually performed improperly. Lay down on a sit-up bench and place your feet under the roller pads. Your knees should be bent so that the angle between your upper and lower legs is about 90 degrees. Fold your arms across your chest (or interlock your fingers behind your head) and lift your head off the bench so that your chin is tucked into your chest. To do the movement, bring your upper torso forward to the mid-range position until it is almost perpendicular to the floor. Pause briefly in this position and then lower yourself under control to the starting position (shoulders near the bench) to obtain a proper stretch. Do not let your head touch the sit-up bench between repetitions. In addition, avoid throwing your arms and/or head forward as you perform the exercise. Once you can perform a set of 12 repetitions in strict form, you can increase the workload on your muscles by holding onto a weight, increasing the incline of the board, performing the exercise more slowly or having someone apply manual resistance to your shoulders.

Crunch

A "crunch" is actually a modified sit-up with a restricted range of motion. Lay down on the floor and place the backs of your lower legs on a bench or a stool. The angle between your upper and lower legs should be about 90 degrees. Placing your legs on a bench or a stool in this manner will relax your iliopsoas muscle, thereby reducing the load on your lumbar spine. Fold your arms across your chest and lift your head off the floor so that your chin is tucked into your chest. (You can also keep your arms flat on the floor at your sides.) To perform the exercise, raise your torso as high as possible to the mid-range position. Pause momentarily in this position and then lower yourself under control to the starting position (shoulders near the floor) to obtain a proper stretch. Once again, do not let your head touch the floor between repetitions. Also, avoid throwing your arms and/or head forward as you do the exercise.

Side Bend

The external and internal obliques are generally the weakest of the abdominal muscles. One of the best movements for exercising the obliques with conventional equipment is a side bend. Stand upright and hold a dumbbell in your right hand at your side. Spread your feet about shoulder-width apart and position your left hand against the left side of your head. Without moving your hips, bend your torso to the right as far as possible. To do the exercise, bring your upper torso to the left as far as possible to the mid-range position. Pause briefly in this position and then return the weight under control to the starting position (torso bent to the right) to ensure an adequate stretch. After performing a set for your left side, repeat the exercise for your right side.

Torso Twist

The obliques may also be strengthened with twisting movements of the trunk. The movement is basically the same as either the sit-up or crunch described previously except that instead of bringing your upper torso directly forward, you would turn or twist your torso to the side during each repetition.

Knee-Up

A knee-up is a productive exercise for training the iliopsoas and the lower portion of the abdominals. Grasp a chin bar, bring your body to a "dead hang" and cross your ankles. To perform the movement, simply bring your knees as close to your chest as possible to the mid-range position. Pause momentarily in this position and then lower your legs under control back to the starting position (legs hanging straight down) to obtain a sufficient stretch. Once you can perform a set of 12 repetitions in strict form, you can increase the workload on your muscles by performing the exercise more slowly or having someone apply manual resistance to your upper legs.

Chapter 14

NECK TRAINING: MAKE AN EFFORT!

Because the neck is not a "show" muscle — like the biceps and triceps — exercises for that area are typically de-emphasized or neglected altogether. Yet, a strong, thickly muscled neck is extremely important in protecting the cervical area from traumatic injury in wrestling and other combative sports such as judo, boxing and football.

Injuries primarily occur when an outside force acting upon a joint momentarily exceeds the structural integrity of that joint such that the muscle and/or tendon has been forcefully stretched or extended beyond its existing range of movement (ROM). Therefore, in order to reduce the potential for neck injury, it is critical that wrestlers strengthen their neck musculature.

BASIC ANATOMY AND MUSCULAR FUNCTION

Regardless of the length of the neck, all mammals — with the exception of several species of sloths — have exactly seven cervical vertebrae. Even a giraffe has seven cervical vertebrae — although each vertebra of the giraffe is about as long as your leg bone! (In a bizarre twist of biological fate, a sparrow has more cervical vertebrae than a giraffe!) In humans, the primary muscles of the neck — namely the sternocleidomastoideus and trapezius — provide support and act to produce a variety of movements.

Your sternocleidomastoideus has two parts or "heads" located on each side of your neck that start behind your ears and run down to your sternum (breastbone) and clavicles (collarbones). When both sides contract at the same time, the sternocleidomastoideus flexes your neck forward thereby bringing your head toward your chest; when one side acts singly, it flexes your neck laterally toward your shoulder or rotates your neck to the side.

Your trapezius is a kite-shaped muscle that covers the uppermost region of your back and the posterior section of your neck. The primary functions of your "traps" are to elevate your shoulders (as in shrugging), to adduct your scapulae (to pinch your shoulder blades together) and to extend your neck backward.

So, these two muscles act upon your neck in eight different ways: (1) flexion of your neck forward; (2) extension of your neck backward; (3,4) lateral flexion of your neck to the left and right; (5,6) rotation of your neck to the left and right; (7) elevation of your shoulders; and (8) adduction of your shoulder blades. In order to develop your neck properly and comprehensively, exercises should be prescribed for as many of the various functions as possible.

GENERAL GUIDELINES

Training your neck requires appropriate EFFORT:

E — Exercise your neck at the beginning of your workout. It is important to devote your full attention to performing exercises for your cervical area. Far too often, the neck is exercised at the end of a workout almost as an afterthought. Instead, you should exercise your neck at the beginning of your workout while you are fresh — both physically as well as psychologically.

F — Focus on doing your repetitions with proper technique. Proper technique is raising the resistance without an excessive use of momentum in about 1-2 seconds, pausing distinctly in the contracted (or mid-range) position and lowering the resistance under control in about 3-4 seconds. This will ensure that the targeted muscles are raising the resistance (rather than momentum) and that your chances of incurring an injury while strength training are minimized. In addition, each repetition should be performed throughout a full ROM. This will allow you to maintain (or perhaps improve) your flexibility and ensure that you are exercising your entire muscle, not just a portion of it.

F — Fatigue your neck muscles within 8-12 repetitions (or 50-70 seconds). A desirable level of fatigue is when you have exhausted your muscles to the point where you literally cannot perform another repetition. Performing sets of less than about 8 repetitions in this exercise increases your risk of injury. Likewise, once you exceed about 12 repetitions, the set becomes an increasingly greater test of aerobic endurance rather than muscular strength.

O — Overload your neck muscles with a workload that is increased steadily and systematically throughout the course of your strength-training program. In order to overload your muscles, you must attempt to increase either the resistance used or the repetitions performed in relation to your previous workout. Each time you attain the maximal number of repetitions, you should increase the resistance during your next workout; if you do not perform the maximal number of repetitions, you should use the same resistance during your next workout but try to increase the number of repetitions.

R — Record the amount of resistance and the number of repetitions you do in your workouts. This is a history of what you accomplished during each and every exercise of each and every strength session. Recording your data can be an extremely valuable tool to monitor your progress and make your workouts more meaningful. This can also be used to identify exercises in which you have reached a plateau. In the unfortunate event of an injury, the effectiveness of your rehabilitative process can be gauged if you have a record of your pre-injury strength levels.

T — Train your neck 2-3 times per week on nonconsecutive days. You should exercise your neck muscles three times per week when not in season and twice per week when in season (but not within 48 hours of a match). Neck exercises should never be done immediately before a practice session or a match.

EXERCISES

The following is a specific description of various exercises that can be performed to strengthen the muscles of your neck using conventional equipment. Unfortunately, it is rare to find a device nowadays to exercise the rotary movement of the neck. Therefore, neck rotation will not be described. However, the same muscle used during neck rotation — the sternocleidomastoideus — is used when performing neck lateral flexion.

Neck Flexion

This exercise works your sternocleidomastoideus (both sides acting together). It is most often performed using machines (selectorized and plate-loaded) or manual resistance. If you are using a machine, adjust the seat so that your face is centered on the head pads when you are sitting upright. Place your feet flat on the floor, grasp the handles and extend your neck backward. If you are using manual resistance, lie supine on a bench, place your feet flat on the floor and position yourself so that your head hangs over the edge. Interlock your fingers and place them across your chest. To do the movement, bring your head as close to your chest as possible to the mid-range position. Pause briefly in this position and then return your head under control back to the starting position (neck extended) to ensure a proper stretch.

Neck Extension

This movement targets your trapezius and neck extensors. It is usually performed using machines (selectorized and plate-loaded) or manual resistance. If you are using a machine, adjust the seat so that the back of your head is centered on the head pads when you are sitting upright. Place your feet flat on the floor, grasp the handles and flex your neck forward. If you are using manual resistance, lie prone on a bench and position yourself so that your head hangs over the edge. Place your hands and feet on the floor (or position your legs across the edge). To do the exercise, extend your neck backward as far as possible to the mid-range position. Pause momentarily in this position and then return your head back to the starting position (chin on chest) to obtain an adequate stretch.

Neck Lateral Flexion

Your sternocleidomastoideus (one side acting singly) is utilized during this movement. This exercise is most often done using machines (selectorized and plate-loaded). Adjust the seat so that the right side of your face is centered on the head pads when you are sitting upright. Place your feet flat on the floor, grasp the handles and position your neck near your left shoulder. To perform the movement, bring your head as close to your right shoulder as possible to the mid-range position (without moving your upper torso). Pause briefly in this position and then return your head back to the starting position (neck near your left shoulder) to provide a proper stretch. After performing a set for the right side of your neck, repeat the exercise for the left side of your neck.

Shoulder Shrug

This is the best exercise for isolating your trapezius muscle. It can be performed with a barbell, dumbbells, trap bar or machines (selectorized and plate-loaded). Use an alternating grip or a grip with both palms facing toward you when using a barbell; use a parallel grip with both palms facing each other when using other equipment. To do the exercise, pull the resistance up as high as possible to the mid-range position (while keeping your arms and legs straight) in an attempt to touch your shoulders to your ears (as if to say, "I don't know"). Pause briefly in this position and then lower the weight back to the starting position (your shoulders away from your ears) to ensure a proper stretch. Avoid throwing the resistance by using your legs or by swinging your upper torso back and forth — movement should only occur around your shoulders. Finally, do not "roll" your shoulders forward or backward as you perform this exercise.

Scapulae Adduction

This exercise for the trapezius is rarely done, yet it is the only one in which adduction of your scapulae is the lone movement. It can be performed with a dumbbell or a seated-row machine (selectorized and plate-loaded). When using a dumbbell, your palm should be facing the bench; when using a machine, use a parallel grip with both palms facing each other. If you are using a dumbbell, place your left hand and your left knee on a bench, position your right foot on the floor at a comfortable distance from the bench and grasp a dumbbell with your right hand. To do the movement, pull the resistance backward as far as possible to the mid-range position in an attempt to touch your shoulder blades together. (Keep your arm perpendicular to the ground.) Pause briefly in this position and then lower the weight back to the starting position (shoulder blades apart) to provide a proper stretch. Avoid throwing the resistance by swinging your upper torso back and forth — movement should only occur around your shoulders. After performing a set for the right side of your body with a dumbbell, repeat the exercise for the left side of your body.

PROTECT THE NECK

Wrestlers who do not perform neck exercises are placing themselves at risk for traumatic injury. Your potential for injury can be greatly reduced with a little EFFORT!

The bench press is perhaps the most popular exercise done in the weight room. What follows are some of the most common questions that coaches and athletes ask about this movement.

Q: Is the bench press a good exercise?

A: The bench press is a very good exercise for the chest, shoulders and triceps. But it is not necessarily more valuable than other movements. Unfortunately, many athletes often spend far too much time performing the bench press while neglecting other important exercises.

Q: How many sets should I have my wrestlers do?

A: Ask five different strength coaches and you are likely to get five different answers. Understand that more is not necessarily better. If more were better, then the best program would have athletes train 24 hours a day. A 1983 study by Stowers and his colleagues compared three groups who trained with either 1 set, 3 sets or 3-5 sets. After seven weeks of training, all three groups increased their one-repetition maximum (1-RM) bench press significantly. In addition, there were no significant differences between the three groups. In effect, the multiple-set groups performed at least three times as many sets (or 200% more) as the one-set group without obtaining a significantly greater increase in their 1-RM bench press.

A program will be productive as long as it is based upon the Overload Principle. There are two main ways that wrestlers can overload their muscles in an exercise: (1) Use more weight than the previous workout and (2) do more repetitions than the previous workout.

Q: How many repetitions should my wrestlers do?

A: A variety of repetition ranges can be used to increase strength in the bench press (as well as other exercises). In the aforementioned study, the three groups trained with as few as 3 repetitions and as many as 12. But remember that performing low-repetition sets increases the risk of injury.

Q: A few of my wrestlers say that their shoulder joints hurt when they do the bench press. Is it okay for them to keep doing the exercise?

A: No. All they are doing is aggravating the condition. You must distinguish between muscle pain and joint pain. Generally speaking, muscle pain is okay. It is simply a sign that high-intensity efforts are being done. On the other hand, joint pain is not okay. It is an indication of probable orthopedic problems. If any of your wrestlers experience pain in their shoulder joints during the bench press, they should modify the exercise. One option is to use a lighter weight and to perform the movement slower than usual. Another possibility is to do the bench press with dumbbells using a parallel grip (in which the palms face each other). If the bench press cannot be done in a pain-free fashion, then it should not be included in the workout. In this case, have your wrestlers do an alternative exercise that addresses the same muscles such as the incline press, decline press or dip.

Q: I can bench press X pounds. Is that good?

A: Unless you are a competitive powerlifter, who cares? Your ability to bench press has absolutely nothing to do with your ability as a wrestler — except if you happen to also compete as a powerlifter. Besides, your ability to bench press is based upon several factors — most of which you simply cannot control. The most obvious factors are the length of your arms and the thickness of your chest. Everything else being equal, an athlete with short arms and a thick chest will be able to bench press more than an athlete with longer arms and a thinner chest.

Q: Is it okay for me to raise my hips when doing the bench press?

A: No it is not. By raising your hips, you are essentially short-ening the distance that the bar must travel to your chest. While this may allow you to lift more weight, it does not mean that you increased your strength. In fact, look at it this way: Suppose that when you keep your hips down, you can bench press 200 pounds a distance of 18 inches — or 3,600 inch-pounds of work [200 pounds x 18 inches]. If you raise your chest to the point where the bar now travels a distance of 15 inches, you would have to bench press 240 pounds just to perform the same amount of work [3,600 inch-pounds divided by 15 inches = 240 pounds].

Q: Should my wrestlers use a wide grip or a narrow grip?

A: Take an empty bar and hold it at shoulder level with your hands spaced far apart. While standing in front of a mirror, press it overhead. Note the distance that the bar traveled vertically. Move your hands closer to your shoulders and try it again. You will find that the narrower grip allowed the bar to travel a greater distance. Being able to move the bar a greater distance means that you had a greater range of motion (ROM) around your shoulder and elbow joints. The greater ROM translates into a greater involvement of your muscle mass. The grip in the bench press should be slightly wider than shoulder-width apart.

Q: Should I lock my elbows between repetitions?

A: Nope. There are two reasons why you should not "lock" or completely extend your elbows. First of all, it unloads your muscles. Second, you increase your risk of hyperextending your elbow joints.

Q: My wrestlers can lift more weight when they bounce the bar off their chests. Is that okay?

A: No! Bouncing the bar off their chests means that they can bounce more weight, not lift more weight. Dropping a barbell onto the chest causes compression. When the musculoskeletal structure "rebounds" or returns to normal, it helps raise the weight. The more you drop the weight, the more rebound you get; the more rebound you get, the less your muscles work; the less your muscles work, the less you increase your strength. Forcefully dropping the bar on the chest also increases the risk of injury to the sternum (breastbone).

Q: What's the difference between a bench press with a barbell and a bench press with a machine?

A. In terms of your response, not much. The bench press — whether done with free weights or machines — addresses the same major muscles: the chest, shoulders and triceps. Although balancing free weights requires a greater involvement of synergistic muscles, it does not appear as if this results in a significantly greater response. Indeed, studies have shown that there are no significant differences in strength development when comparing groups who used free weights and groups who used machines. The bottom line is that your muscles do not have eyes, brains or cognitive ability. Therefore, they cannot possibly know whether the source of resistance is a barbell, dumbbells, a selectorized machine, a plate-loaded machine or another human being. The sole factors that determine your response from weight training are your genetic makeup and your level of effort — not the equipment that you used.

Chapter 16
LOSING FAT:HIGH INTENSITY
OR LOW INTENSITY?

Which is the most effective method for losing fat: high-intensity exercise or low-intensity exercise? This question has lead to a notion that is well meaning but not supported by scientific evidence.

ENERGY SOURCES

During activity, there are three possible sources of energy (or fuel) available for you to use: carbohydrate, fat and protein. Of these three energy sources, your body does not like to use protein as a fuel. In fact, protein is used as a last resort. Remember, protein is located in your muscles and if you are in a situation where you must rely on it as an energy source, then you are literally eating yourself to death. So that leaves you with carbohydrate and fat as your main energy sources.

Exactly which energy source is preferred during activity is based upon the level of intensity (or effort) that is required. During exercise of relatively high intensity, a greater percentage of carbohydrate is used as an energy source; during exercise of relatively low intensity, a greater percentage of fat is used as an energy source. (Carbohydrate is a more efficient source of energy. However, fat is used as an energy source because your body does not need to be efficient at lower levels of intensity.)

This is not to say that carbohydrate and fat are the sole sources of energy during activities of high and low intensity. Rather, they are both used but to different degrees: During high-intensity activity, carbohydrate is the principal energy source but fat is also used; during low-intensity activity, fat is the principal energy source but carbohydrate is also used.

These physiological facts have led to the mistaken belief that

81

low-intensity (or "fat-burning") exercise is better than high-intensity (or "carbohydrate-burning") exercise when it comes to "burning" fat as well as expending calories and losing weight. Furthermore, this misconception has spawned the hyped-up notion that people should exercise within their "fat-burning zones."

CALORIC EXPENDITURE

The concept of keeping the exercise intensity low in order to mobilize and selectively utilize a higher percentage of fat may sound logical but it does not hold up mathematically and has never been verified in a laboratory setting. In truth, even though a greater percentage of calories come from fat during low-intensity exercise, a greater number of fat calories (and total calories) are expended during high-intensity exercise.

During any activity, your rate of caloric expenditure is directly related to your intensity of effort — the higher your intensity, the greater your rate of caloric expenditure. In the case of running, for example, your intensity is directly associated with your speed — the faster you run, the greater the rate of caloric expenditure. The time of your activity is also a factor — the longer that you perform a given activity, the greater the total caloric expenditure.

The American College of Sports Medicine offers equations for determining oxygen consumption and caloric expenditure during walking (an activity of relatively low intensity) and running (an activity of relatively high intensity). Based upon these equations, a 165-pound man who walks three miles in 60 minutes will utilize roughly 4.33 calories per minute (cal/min). Over the course of his 60-minute walk, his total caloric usage would be about 260 calories [4.33 cal/min x 60 min]. If that same individual ran those three miles in 30 minutes, he would use about 13.38 cal/min. (Note the higher rate of caloric expenditure.) During his 30-minute effort, he would have used about 401 total calories [13.38 cal/min x 30 min]. So exercising at a higher level of intensity utilized significantly more calories than exercising at a lower level of intensity [401 cal compared to 260 cal]. This is true despite the fact that the activity of lower intensity was performed for twice as long as the activity of higher intensity [60 min compared to 30 min].

These calculations have been corroborated by research performed in the laboratory. In one study, a group of subjects walked on a treadmill at an average speed of 3.8 miles per hour (mph) for 30 minutes. In this instance, the subjects used an average of about 8 cal/min for a total caloric expenditure of 240 calories [8 cal/min x 30 min]. Of these 240 calories, 59% [144 cal] were from carbohydrate and 41% [96 cal] were from fat. As part of the study, the same group also ran on a treadmill at an average speed of 6.5 mph for 30 minutes. At this relatively higher level of intensity, the subjects used an average of about 15 cal/min for a total caloric expenditure of 450 calories [15 cal/min x 30 min]. Of these 450 calories, 76% [342 cal] were from carbohydrate and 24% [108 cal] were from fat. In other words, exercising at a higher level of intensity resulted in a greater total caloric expenditure than exercising at a lower level of intensity [450 cal versus 240 cal] and also used a greater number of calories from fat in the same length of time [108 cal compared to 96 cal]. Additional studies have also demonstrated that more calories are expended when running a given distance than walking the same distance.

THE BOTTOM LINE

The intent behind advocating low-intensity exercise of long duration is to enhance safety and improve compliance in the non-athletic population. However, low-intensity exercise is not more effective for fat loss — or weight loss — than high-intensity exercise. Suppose, however, that low-intensity activity was better for losing fat and weight. Since activities of the lowest intensity require the greatest percentage of fat as the energy source, this would suggest that the best activity for fat/weight loss would be sleeping.

In terms of losing weight, more calories must be expended than consumed in order to produce a caloric deficit. Whether carbohydrate or fat is used to produce this caloric shortfall is immaterial. A caloric deficit created by the selective use of fat as an energy source does not necessarily translate into greater fat loss compared to an equal caloric deficit created by the use of carbohydrate as an energy source.

Researchers who perform studies and review the scientific literature in the area of exercise and weight management generally agree that it probably does not matter whether you use fat or carbohydrate while exercising in order to lose weight. Finally, it should also be noted that low-intensity exercise usually does not elevate the heart rate enough to improve your level of aerobic fitness.

So, whether you are strength training, conditioning or drilling, you should use the highest possible level of effort. Make hard work a standard part of your athletic lifestyle. And that's the bottom line.

Chapter 17
ANATOMY OF A
STRETCHING PROGRAM

Flexibility can be defined as the range of motion (ROM) throughout which your joints can move. The best way for you to maintain — or improve — the ROM of your joints is to perform specific flexibility movements to stretch the surrounding muscles. Flexibility movements are undoubtedly the simplest and most effortless physical activity that you can perform — the exertion level is quite low and relaxation is an absolute requirement. Nevertheless, many athletes often overlook or underemphasize their flexibility training.

Increasing your flexibility serves several purposes. First of all, becoming more flexible generally makes you less susceptible to injury. Secondly, being more flexible enables you to exert your strength over a greater ROM. Finally, stretching your muscles is a way of relieving and/or reducing general muscle soreness that may result from unfamiliar activities or intense workouts.

FACTORS AFFECTING FLEXIBILITY

There are many factors that affect your ROM — some of which you have little or no control over. For example, there is a distinct relationship between your age and the degree of your flexibility. The greatest increase in flexibility usually occurs up to and between the ages of 7 and 12. During early adolescence, flexibility tends to level off and thereafter begins to decline with increasing age. Therefore, one of the goals of your flexibility program is to slow or perhaps reverse this decline.

To a degree, your flexibility is also related to your gender. Although some males are more flexible than some females, males are generally less flexible than females.

In addition, it is important to understand that your flexibility is affected by several genetic or inherited characteristics such as the insertion points of your muscles and your ratio of muscle-to-fat — that is, excessive body fat. Your ROM also has genetic structural limitations including your bones, tendons, ligaments and skin along with the extensibility of your muscles.

Previous injury to a muscle or connective tissue may also affect your ROM. Furthermore, immobilizing a joint during rehabilitation may cause your connective tissue to adapt to its shortest functional length thereby reducing the ROM of the joint.

Finally, your body temperature is another factor that influences joint flexibility. Muscles and connective tissue that are warmed up will be more flexible and extensible than muscles and connective tissue that are not warmed up.

ASSESSING FLEXIBILITY

Because your ROM is affected by the aforementioned factors, it is difficult to assess flexibility in a fair manner. In addition, some measurements of flexibility can be misleading. A perfect example of this is the traditional sit-and-reach test in which a person sits down and reaches as far as possible. This test is often used to measure the flexibility of the lower back and the hamstrings. However, a sit-and-reach test does not take into consideration limb lengths. Everything else being equal, those with long arms and/or short legs have a distinct biomechanical advantage in a sit-and-reach test. These individuals may appear to be flexible but may actually be quite inflexible. Conversely, those with short arms and/or long legs have a distinct biomechanical disadvantage in a sit-and-reach test. These individuals may appear to be inflexible but may really be quite flexible. In the case of a sit-and-reach test, measuring the angle of flexion between the lumbar spine and the upper legs with a goniometer yields a fairer appraisal of flexibility. (A goniometer is a protractor-like instrument with two movable arms that enable you to measure joint angles.)

Lastly, it should be noted that your flexibility is joint-specific — a high degree of flexibility in one joint does not necessarily indicate high flexibility in other joints. Along these lines, it would not be uncommon for your flexibility to vary from one side of your body to the other.

In short, the purpose of assessing flexibility should not be to compare your performance to that of someone else. Flexibility assessments are much more meaningful when your present flexibility is compared to your past flexibility.

"WARMING UP"

The research regarding the need for a "warm up" seems to be inconclusive. Some studies have shown that a warm up facilitates performance; other studies have shown that performances without a prior warm up are no different than those with a warm up. Nevertheless, a warm up has both physiological and psychological importance.

For years, warming up was synonymous with stretching. However, warming up and stretching are two separate entities and must be treated as such. A warm up is meant to prepare you for an upcoming activity. On the other hand, the purpose of stretching is to induce a more long-term change in your ROM.

A warm up should precede your flexibility training. Warm-up activities usually consist of low-intensity movements such as light jogging or calisthenics. Regardless of the warm-up activity, the idea is to systematically increase your body temperature and the blood flow to your muscles. Breaking a light sweat during the warm up indicates that your body temperature has been raised sufficiently and that you are ready to begin stretching your muscles. As noted previously, muscles and connective tissue that are warmed up have increased flexibility and extensibility. (In all likelihood, when the environmental temperature is high your body temperature is already elevated sufficiently to start stretching.)

Your biological tissue is most extensible at the end of an activity when your body temperature is elevated. Because of this, some authorities recommend that stretching should be performed *after* you have completed an activity. This may also reduce general muscle soreness after an intense activity.

By the way, there is no need for you to warm up or stretch prior to strength training — provided that a relatively high number of repetitions are performed and the weight is lifted in a controlled manner. However, warming up prior to an activity involving rapid muscle contractions — such as drilling or sprinting — is advisable to reduce your risk of injury.

SEVEN STRETCHING STRATEGIES

Though your level of flexibility may be limited by one or more of the factors previously mentioned, you can improve your ROM through an organized stretching program. Like all other forms of exercise, stretching movements have certain guidelines that must be followed in order to make the stretches safe and effective. Adopting these guidelines permits you to maintain or improve your current ROM. Additionally, you will be less likely to get injured and will perform closer to your performance potential.

1. STRETCH under control without bouncing, bobbing or jerking movements. Bouncing during the stretch actually makes the movement more painful and increases your risk of muscle soreness and tissue damage.

2. INHALE and EXHALE normally during the stretch without holding your breath. Holding your breath elevates your blood pressure which disrupts your balance and breathing mechanisms.

3. STRETCH comfortably in a pain-free manner. Since pain is an indication that you are stretching at or near your structural limits, you should only stretch to a point of mild discomfort.

4. RELAX during the stretch. Relaxing mentally and physically allows you to stretch your muscles throughout a greater ROM.

5. HOLD the stretched position for 30-60 seconds. Gradually stretching your muscles to a point of mild discomfort, holding that position and then gradually returning them to their pre-stretched state enables you to stretch farther with little risk of pain or injury.

6. ATTEMPT to stretch a little bit farther than the last time. Progressively increasing your ROM — and the time that each stretch is held — improves your flexibility.

7. PERFORM flexibility movements on a regular basis. You should stretch at least once a day, especially before a practice, match, conditioning workout or any other activity that involves explosive, ballistic movements.

FLEXIBILITY EXERCISES

Although your body has roughly 200 joints, it is not necessary to perform a flexibility movement for each one. Your joints range from those that are relatively immovable (e.g., the sutures of your skull) to those that are freely movable (e.g., your hips and elbows). You can stretch your muscles in a comprehensive manner by simply performing flexibility movements for your major muscles: your hips, groin (the inner thigh), hamstrings, quadriceps, calves, dorsi flexors, chest, upper back (the "lats"), shoulders, biceps, triceps, abdominals and lower back. There are numerous stretches with many variations that address these muscle groups. As such, your stretching program can be individualized to meet your personal preferences.

Chapter 18

THE SAFE WEIGHT ROOM
— PART I

Strength training — like any other sport or activity — contains the potential for injury. Safety in the weight room, however, extends far beyond the scope of spotters and collars. Indeed, a safe program may be a coach's only defense against a lawsuit.

Nowadays, most universities have at least one strength coach on staff who is responsible for the strength training of the varsity athletes. In many cases, the "strength staff" is large enough such that one or more of them are assigned specifically to priority sports such as wrestling. At most high schools and even some colleges, however, a professionally trained strength coach is not on the staff. In these instances, the strength training of athletes is often supervised by one of the team's coaches. Sometimes, coaches who have little or no background in the safe operation of a weight room suddenly find themselves supervising an area of high liability. Therefore, the intent of this information is to provide coaches with a basic understanding of their legal responsibilities in the weight room.

NEGLIGENCE

In simple terms, negligence is when a coach fails to act as a reasonable and prudent coach would act in a similar situation. If you are sued and brought to trail, a judge or jury determines the appropriateness of your actions. Four factors are considered in deciding whether or not a coach is negligent. All four of these factors must be present to determine negligence.

The first factor is that there must be the presence of a duty. As coaches, we have a number of legal duties. (These duties will be explained shortly.) Secondly, one of the duties must have been violated. A third factor is whether your breach of duty was responsible for an athlete's injuries. Finally, the damages or injuries are considered.

Again, all four of these factors must be proven before you can be found negligent. You will not be found negligent if any of these factors are absent.

LEGAL DUTIES

As coaches, we have certain legal obligations to our athletes that must be performed reasonably and prudently. According to the law, we are expected to provide several major duties for our athletes. These duties involve three main areas of responsibility: supervision, environment and the selection and conduct of activities.

Supervision

First, we must provide adequate supervision. Supervision is one of our most important responsibilities since it includes all of our legal duties.

To begin with, you should be qualified to supervise a weight room. Just because you have 18-inch arms or a 400-pound bench press does not automatically mean that you are a qualified supervisor. There are various certifications in strength training but a few of these programs test you on their particular approach (which is often biased and sometimes dangerous). For example, one national certification test includes questions on the latest Eastern European training methodology. However, most of you are coaching wrestlers not aspiring Bulgarian weightlifters! So you do not necessarily need to possess a certification but you should be mature, competent, knowledgeable and understand your legal duties. If you have assistants, make sure they are qualified as well.

In performing your supervisory responsibilities, you must position yourself so that you can see and hear as much as possible. If you are the only supervisor in the weight room, try not to focus all of your attention on one athlete. Likewise, you cannot supervise properly if you are lifting weights while your wrestlers are lifting weights. Do not coach from behind your desk either — get out on the floor with your athletes.

Obviously, you cannot supervise if you are not there! If one of your wrestlers gets hurt while you are gone, you could be found negligent if it was determined that your absence contributed to the injury. In short, you are asking for a lot of trouble by leaving your athletes unattended in the weight room.

Providing a Safe Environment

It is your legal duty to provide and maintain a safe weight room with good equipment in proper condition. You are responsible for eliminating any hazardous conditions or informing your supervisor of the situation in writing. You are also responsible for noticing what a reasonable and a prudent coach should have noticed whether you did or not.

A safe weight room starts with safe equipment. Insist that your Athletic Department purchase the best equipment that its budget allows. Inspect the equipment regularly and thoroughly — especially any moving parts — to ensure that it is in good working order. Defective equipment should be replaced or removed. You should position the equipment in the weight room so that there is enough space for your athletes to move around without getting hurt. Insist that your athletes return all plates and dumbbells to their proper places. Your athletes should also be required to use a spotter and collars during any overhead lifts such as the bench press, incline press and seated press.

THE SAFE WEIGHT ROOM 19
— PART II

Previously, negligence and its determining factors were described. Additionally, two of the three main areas of a coach's responsibility in the weight room were discussed: providing adequate supervision and a safe environment. The following information will focus on the third main area of responsibility: the selection and conduct of activities.

SELECTION AND CONDUCT OF ACTIVITIES

This responsibility is divided into preparation and planning, warning of risks, evaluating athletes for limitations, equal pairing of athletes and first aid and medical procedure.

Preparation and Planning

You cannot simply open the doors to the weight room and "wing it." Planning begins with your approach to strength training.

First and foremost, your program should be safe. If your main purpose in strength training is to reduce an athlete's risk of injury, it becomes both contradictory as well as unwise to advocate unsafe lifting methods. Require your wrestlers to perform each repetition in a deliberate, controlled manner throughout a full range of motion. Do not allow them to explode with a weight since this exposes their joints and connective tissues to enormous forces that may cause an immediate injury or predispose them to a later injury. Also, avoid any potentially dangerous exercises or activities — such as the barbell squat, power clean, snatch and plyometrics — that place excessive strain on their musculoskeletal systems.

Secondly, your approach should be practical. Asking your

athletes to lift four days a week on a split routine while doing 30 sets each workout is not very reasonable especially if you have 40 wrestlers on your squad. Do not emphasize one-repetition maximum lifts either; just because your athletes can lift a lot of weight for one repetition does not mean that they are suddenly better wrestlers. Remember, you are not training a weightlifting team. In addition, your athletes should not spend an inordinate amount of time bench pressing. Make sure your program addresses all of the body's major muscle groups and require your wrestlers to perform neck-strengthening exercises as a safeguard against cervical injury.

Your program should also be efficient. Although split routines, pyramiding, periodization and other competitive-lifting techniques certainly can be effective, they are not usually economical in terms of the time that is spent. Your athletes should strive to obtain the maximal results in the minimal amount of time.

Finally, your program should be productive. It makes little sense to have your wrestlers engage in strength training if your approach does not yield favorable results.

There are a few additional points to consider in your planning. You should schedule an orientation meeting or a strength-training clinic in which your athletes receive information concerning sound strength-training fundamentals. They should also be given instruction in using the equipment properly and safely. In addition, you should explain the potential risks of injury due to utilizing poor lifting techniques (and frequently remind your athletes while they are lifting).

When your wrestlers begin your strength program, give them a brief, basic routine. This will give them time to adapt to the intensity of your program and enable them to understand more of what they are expected to accomplish. To avoid possible injury, have your athletes increase their resistance by about 5% or less when they perform the maximal number of repetitions. It is important that the increase in weight be relative, not absolute. For instance, if one of your wrestlers was able to bench press 200 pounds, a 10-pound jump for the next workout would be a 5% increase in weight; on the other hand, if he's curling 40 pounds, that same 10-pound jump would represent a 25% increase in weight which may invite injury.

Coaches must determine how many athletes they can adequately and safely supervise based upon staff, equipment, time, space and experience. So if you are to supervise by yourself, do not schedule 40 athletes to lift at the same time in a cramped 1000-square-foot facility that is only equipped with two barbells and one Universal Multi-Gym.

Lastly, do not merely keep abreast of current strength-training information — read it critically to determine if it is indeed safe, practical, efficient and productive. Be wary of routines that are based primarily on either personal anecdotes or biased research. You should also keep in mind that strength programs can be advocated by individuals whose sole purpose is financial gain.

Warning of Risks

You may be found negligent if you do not sufficiently warn your athletes of the risks involved in lifting weights. Your warnings should be clear and repeated as often as is necessary to ensure compliance.

Your athletes can only assume those risks that are inherent to weight training. For example, there is always a possibility that a weight could be accidentally dropped on someone's foot or that someone's finger could get caught in a machine. If you do not warn your wrestlers of this possibility, however, they may not be responsible. Furthermore, athletes should not assume the risk of any improper techniques or potentially dangerous exercises that are recommended by their coach.

Although some equipment manufacturers have placed warning labels on their products such as "KEEP HANDS AWAY WHILE MACHINE IS IN USE" and "DO NOT USE WITHOUT PROPER SUPERVISION," you must still ensure that your athletes have read and understand the warnings.

Finally, provide your athletes with a written set of rules governing the use of the facility and make certain that they understand the content. Persistent disregard for the rules should be dealt with by suspension of lifting privileges.

Evaluating Athletes for Limitations

You have a legal duty to make sure that your athletes are physically able to strength train in a safe manner. You can use the team physician and/or athletic trainer as your resources to determine any restrictions on lifting. By all means, require your athletes to obtain a comprehensive medical examination each year before engaging in a strength-training program or a re-evaluation for return after an injury.

Equal Pairing of Athletes

You also have a legal responsibility to pair your athletes so that none of them is placed at a gross disadvantage in terms of size, weight or maturation. Imagine if one of your athletes got injured on the bench press because the partner you assigned was physically unable to spot a heavy barbell. Additionally, matching your athletes properly will decrease the likelihood of one wrestler injuring another during a partner- or manual-resistance exercise.

First Aid and Emergency Medical Procedures

When performed, this is your most important legal responsibility. Whenever an athlete under your supervision is injured, you must provide reasonable medical assistance as soon as possible. This requires basic first-aid skills and a system of obtaining trained medical personnel as quickly as possible. Unless you are adequately trained, do not go beyond basic first-aid treatment. In carrying out this duty, you can be found negligent if you do nothing, select the wrong action or perform improper medical care.

It is recommended that you review and/or renew your first-aid and CPR skills as needed. Keep the telephone numbers of the school nurse and an ambulance near the phone. You should also have a first-aid kit in the weight room that contains sterile dressings, tape, bandages and so on. Lastly, an injury report should be made in the event of a serious injury.

CONCLUDING REMARKS

The subject of drug abuse merits separate discussion. It is unethical for coaches to recommend or distribute anabolic steroids, human growth hormones or any other illegal drug to their athletes. Distributing illicit drugs is also a felony, coaches. Moreover, deaths directly attributed to steroid abuse are now being documented. If you recommend steroids to an athlete and life-threatening symptoms occur, you could be sued and brought to trial because of gross negligence on your part.

It has often been said that "anybody can sue anyone for anything." This may be true but coaches can go a long way in decreasing their chances of being sued by understanding their legal duties and operating their weight rooms in a safe and competent manner. Use your common sense — you owe it to yourself and especially to your athletes.

Chapter 20

THE CREATINE MYTH: A REBUTTAL — PART I

The April 15, 2000 issue of *Wrestling USA* magazine featured an article entitled "The Creatine Myth" which was written by Steven Plisk. Early in his article, Mr. Plisk stated that "coaches, parents and athletes need to have accurate information about creatine." While there is total agreement with this specific statement, there is considerable disagreement with much of the "information about creatine" that Mr. Plisk presented as "accurate."

IS CREATINE EFFECTIVE?

Mr. Plisk noted that "[wrestlers] are aware of the solid research showing that [creatine] increases strength, improves endurance, and builds lean muscle mass." What does the "solid research" really say about the effects of creatine on these three variables? But perhaps more importantly for coaches and wrestlers, what does the "solid research" say about the effects of creatine during the performance of actual sports, realistic events or competitive situations?

Does It Increase Strength?

While it is true that there is "solid research" showing that creatine "increases strength," Mr. Plisk failed to mention that there is roughly an equal amount of "solid research" showing that it does not produce significant increases in strength or other strength-related measures. For example, a 1996 study using 9 subjects showed that creatine did not increase maximal isometric strength of the quadriceps. A 1997 study involving 34 football and track athletes found that creatine did not significantly improve low-body strength or one-repetition maximum (1-RM) strength in the bench press. Another 1997 study using 20 athletes revealed that creatine did not affect 1-RM strength in elbow flexion, peak velocity (of the shoulder) or torque. Yet another 1997 study involving 24 football players showed that creatine (and a glucose supplement) did not significantly increase 1-RM strength in the bench press or performance in the vertical jump. A fourth 1997 study using 36 track athletes found that creatine did not significantly improve performance in the vertical jump. A 1998 study involving 44 subjects revealed that creatine did not improve 1-RM strength in the bench press. Another 1998 study using 14 athletes showed that creatine did not significantly improve performance in the vertical jump. A third 1998 study involving 25 football players found that creatine did not significantly improve squat or power clean lifting volume. A 1999 study using 16 physical-education students showed that creatine did not alter the rate of maximal force production. A 2000 study involving 23 subjects determined that creatine did not improve peak torque of the quadriceps. Another 2000 study using 30 subjects found that creatine did not significantly improve handgrip strength.

Taking into account this and other "solid research," the effect of creatine on strength and other strength-related measures is inconclusive.

Does It Improve Endurance?

Considering the fact that creatine is an energy substrate used during maximal, short-term efforts with essentially no role during long-term efforts, it would not be expected that it "improves endurance." And, in fact, there is very little "solid research" showing that creatine has any positive effect on endurance other than during activities that involve *repeated* maximal, short-term efforts. Even Dr. Richard Kreider — a well-known proponent of creatine supplementation and an associate of Mr. Plisk — admits that "creatine supplementation does not appear to enhance endurance exercise."

Does It Build Lean-Muscle Mass?

What many studies have shown is that creatine can increase body mass, not *lean*-body mass (LBM) or lean-muscle mass. And

99

the most likely reason for the increased body mass is primarily due to water retention (within skeletal muscle cells) that — needless to say — is not necessarily desirable.

The truth of the matter is that there is no pill, powder or potion currently in existence that, by itself, "builds lean-muscle mass" in healthy individuals. None. There is only one thing that "builds lean-muscle mass": exercise. When *combined* with exercise — particularly progressive-resistance exercise — some studies found that creatine increased LBM. In all cases, the subjects in those studies were engaged in some type of strength-training activity. Interestingly, a 1997 study showed that a group who used creatine increased their LBM by 4.8 kilograms while a group who took a placebo increased their LBM by 3.5 kilograms. Moreover, it is important to note that the LBM of the subjects in this study was *estimated* by skinfold measurements — an assessment that can be greatly influenced by varying degrees of human error.

Finally, numerous studies have shown that creatine — even when used in conjunction with progressive-resistance exercise — failed to significantly increase LBM. Therefore, the "solid research" examining the effect of creatine on LBM is inconclusive.

Does It Improve Athletic Performance?

Much of the research investigating creatine — including that which has been mentioned earlier — has been done in an extremely well-controlled environment, namely a laboratory. In a controlled laboratory setting, the best evidence for performance enhancement from the use of creatine is in repeated maximal, short-term sprints on a stationary bicycle (and even then, some studies have shown no improvements). Unfortunately, there are no competitions for repeated maximal, short-term sprints on a stationary bicycle. Of the research that has been done outside a laboratory — or "in the field" — very few studies have shown that creatine had any beneficial effects during the performance of actual sports, realistic events or competitive situations. Simply consider the following studies — many of which used highly trained athletes:

As of 1998, a total of five studies had investigated the effects of creatine on actual sports performance *done outside a laboratory* in high-intensity efforts lasting 30 seconds or less. All five studies found no significant improvements in performance from creatine supplementation. For example, a 1996 study involving 32 elite male and female swimmers from the Australian National Team showed that creatine did not enhance performance in swim sprints of 25 and 50 meters. Another 1996 study using 20 male and female swimmers found that creatine actually *worsened* performance in swim sprints of 25 and 50 meters. Yet another 1996 study involving 24 highly trained athletes revealed that creatine did not enhance running velocity in a 60-meter sprint. A 1997 study using 34 football and track athletes showed that creatine did not significantly improve performance in a 40-yard dash. Another 1997 study involving 24 football players found that creatine did not significantly improve performance in a 100-yard dash.

As of 1998, a total of seven studies (including two that were also mentioned in the previous paragraph) had investigated the effects of creatine on actual sports performance *done outside a laboratory* in efforts lasting 30-150 seconds. Six of the seven studies found no significant improvements in performance from creatine supplementation. For instance, two 1996 studies using a total of 52 elite male and female swimmers found that creatine did not improve performance in a 100-meter swim. A 1997 study involving 12 trained female runners showed that creatine did not improve performance in a 700-meter run A 1998 study using 24 U. S. Navy Special Warfare personnel (SEALs) determined that creatine did not significantly improve the time taken to complete an obstacle course (which took roughly two minutes).

As of 1998, a total of four studies had investigated the effects of creatine on actual sports performance *done outside a laboratory* in long-term efforts lasting more than 150 seconds. Three of the four studies found no significant improvements in performance from creatine supplementation. Actually, a 1993 study using 18 well-trained male runners showed that creatine produced significantly *slower* times in a 6,000-meter run. Additionally, a 1996 study involving 13 cyclists found that creatine did not increase the distance cycled in one hour.

To summarize: As of 1998, a total of 14 different studies had investigated the effects of creatine on actual sports performance *done outside a laboratory* in efforts ranging from a handful of seconds to more than 150 seconds. In 12 of the 14 studies, creatine supplementation did not produce significant improvements in performance. Collectively, this "solid research" shows that any improved performance that *may* occur in laboratory settings does not translate into improved performance in realistic situations. This is especially true of highly trained or elite athletes.

THE CREATINE MYTH: A REBUTTAL — PART II

The April 15, 2000 issue of *Wrestling USA* magazine featured an article entitled "The Creatine Myth" which was written by Steven Plisk. In his article, Mr. Plisk endorsed the safety (and effectiveness) of creatine supplementation.

IS CREATINE SAFE?

Mr. Plisk stated that "despite extensive and expanding use, no scientific studies have reported any negative side affects [sic]." This statement, in itself, is quite puzzling. While there certainly has been "extensive and expanding use" of creatine, it has absolutely nothing to do with what has been reported in "scientific studies" with respect to "negative side [e]ffects." Be that as it may, the fact of the matter is that there have not been any adverse side effects reported in studies using 20-30 grams of creatine per day for up to seven days. Nor have there been any adverse side effects reported in studies using smaller dosages of 2-3 grams of creatine per day for longer periods up to seven weeks. However, this is nowhere near the months — or years — that an athlete might use creatine. Countless scientific, medical and nutritional authorities agree that the long-term effects of creatine supplementation are unknown. In fact, a 1998 study — co-authored by Mr. Plisk — stated that "little data are available evaluating the medical safety of supplementing the diet with creatine during training for prolonged periods of time." There is also a concern that many individuals typically exceed the "recommended dosage" — undoubtedly putting them at greater risk for incurring negative side effects.

And while there have been no adverse side effects reported in scientific studies conducted in a laboratory setting, those of us "in the trenches" have heard an endless exchange of anecdotal accounts from around the world concerning athletes who have taken creatine and experienced an abundance of adverse side effects. Although these observations are anecdotal, their sheer volume is such that they cannot be ignored. It is also important to consider a 1999 study published in a peer-reviewed journal that surveyed 52 baseball and football players who voluntarily took creatine. Of the 52 athletes, 14 (26.9%) did not report any adverse effects. Stated otherwise, 38 (73.1%) reported at least one adverse side effect.

Due to individual variability, some may be more susceptible to adverse side effects than others. However, the following potential side effects are of greatest concern:

Water Retention

During the first few days of the "loading phase," there is an increase in the retention of water within muscle cells and a concomitant — and significant — decrease in the production of urine. As noted earlier in this rebuttal, the retention of water probably accounts for the rapid increase in body mass that accompanies creatine supplementation. In all likelihood, a rapid increase in body mass would hinder performance in mass-dependent activities such as running and swimming. In addition, unintentional weight gain may be a concern for wrestlers and other competitive athletes who must "make weight."

Intracellular water retention would also result in muscle enlargement. This muscular hypertrophy is transient, however, and unrelated to the long-term, adaptive increases in muscular size that occur in response to progressive-resistance exercise.

Muscle Cramping

One of the most frequently reported side effects of creatine supplementation outside a laboratory is muscle cramping — which is often described as being "severe." In the aforementioned 1999 survey, 13 of the 52 athletes (25.0%) who used creatine reported muscle cramps. The large fluid shift into skeletal muscle (intracellular water retention) that is caused by creatine supplementation is thought to dilute electrolytes, thereby increasing the potential for muscle cramps. If creatine does induce an electrolyte imbalance, athletes who are not well hydrated and/or are training intensely in hot, humid environments where sweat rates are high would have a greater-than-normal risk of muscle cramping.

Dehydration/Heat-Related Illness

In 1998, the wrestling community was shocked by the deaths of three wrestlers in a period of 32 days: Freshman Billy Jack Saylor of Campbell University (North Carolina) on November 7, senior Joseph LaRosa of Wisconsin-LaCrosse on November 21 and junior Jeff Reese of the University of Michigan on December 9. One common thread connecting the wrestlers is that all three died while trying to lose a fairly substantial amount of weight in a relatively short period of time. The manner in which all three attempted to lose weight was certainly unsafe and they were severely dehydrated. But the methods that they used in an attempt to lose weight had been quite commonplace in wrestling: restricting food and fluid intakes, wearing "sauna suits" and exercising in hot environments. Yet, there is no record of a similar death in collegiate wrestling. Actually, according to the National Collegiate Athletic Association (NCAA) there is *no* other instance of *any* college wrestler *ever* dying in *any* manner. Think about it: No deaths in a period of about one century and then three in a period of about one month. The Centers for Disease Control and Prevention determined that the wrestlers died because they "used vapor-impermeable suits and exercised vigorously in hot environments" which "promoted dehydration and heat-related illness."

At the time of their deaths, many quickly pointed an accusatory finger at creatine. The reason is that one of the most commonly reported side effects related to the use of creatine is dehydration. In the previously noted 1999 survey, 7 of the 52 athletes (13.5%) who took creatine reported dehydration. Ironically, the increased water retention within muscle cells that is associated with the use of creatine increases the risk of dehydration and heat-related illness. This is because the fluid shift into skeletal muscle reduces blood plasma volume which, in turn, reduces the ability to dissipate heat. Although it was not linked to the deaths of the wrestlers, some believe that creatine could intensify an already dehydrated state, resulting in heightened thermal stress and a resultant life-threatening situation.

Muscle Strains/Dysfunction

It is speculated that the intracellular water retention related to the use of creatine increases the intramuscular pressure which could contribute to muscle strains and/or dysfunction.

Gastrointestinal Distress

Creatine may cause a variety of gastrointestinal disturbances. In the aforementioned 1999 survey, 16 of the 52 athletes (30.8%) who used creatine reported diarrhea. Other gastrointestinal afflictions that are often cited anecdotally include an upset stomach, gastrointestinal pain, flatulence, nausea and vomiting.

Liver Function

Research has shown that when the consumption of exogenous (foreign) creatine is increased, the production of endogenous (natural) creatine by the liver is decreased. It is unclear as to how the long-term use of creatine might influence the function of the liver with respect to endogenous creatine synthesis.

Kidney Function

There is a limit as to how much creatine can be extracted from the bloodstream and stored in muscle. Once this saturation point is reached, additional amounts are excreted by the kidneys. Creatine supplementation can produce astronomical increases in the urinary excretion rate of creatine. In a 1997 study, subjects ingested 20 grams of creatine per day for five days (a typical "recommended dosage" during the "loading phase") and — in comparison to their "placebo condition" — experienced an average elevation in their urinary excretion rates of 8,856.7%. The percentage of this "massive urine excretion" — in the words of the authors — may have been even greater since this study only used a two-week "washout" period which may not have been enough time to normalize the baseline readings for the placebo condition. There is concern that the increased urinary excretion rate of creatine places excessive strain on the kidneys.

A 1998 study using 25 "healthy" football players found that 28 days of creatine supplementation (15.75 grams per day) produced changes in muscle and liver enzymes — which are often used as indicators or "markers" of kidney (and liver) function. In this study — co-authored by Mr. Plisk — a group who took creatine experienced increases in the levels of four enzymes of 16.5, 16.6, 24.1 and 155.5%. (Astonishingly, the researchers somehow referred to this as a "mild elevation.") In comparison, a group who took a placebo experienced increases in the levels of two enzymes of 11.4 and 70.1% and *decreases* in the levels of two enzymes of 2.4 and 7.4%. (Analysis of a fifth enzyme showed a very slight elevation in both groups.) Further, two reports of the same 1996 study showed that eight weeks of creatine supplementation (20 grams per day for five days and 10 grams per day for 51 days) produced significant elevations in muscle and liver enzymes. Although the elevated levels returned to normal following a four-week withdrawal of creatine, it still raises fears — particularly for individuals with impaired kidney (or liver) function.

Case in point: In 1998, a 25-year-old soccer player with a history of kidney disease experienced a sudden and substantial deterioration of his condition while taking creatine. After being advised to stop taking creatine, his kidney function returned to normal. Incidentally, his intake of creatine did not exceed the "recommended dosage." Also in 1998, three physicians reported "renal insufficiency" — a functional disorder of the kidneys — in a 19-year-old football player that was induced by regular creatine supplementation. Although his intake of creatine exceeded the "recommended dosage," the grim reality is that many athletes routinely do the same. The physicians who authored this report recommended that athletes who use creatine should have their kidney function assessed.

The sole end product of the breakdown of creatine is creatinine. Serum creatinine is used indirectly as an indicator of kidney stress. The previously mentioned 1998 study — in which Mr. Plisk was a co-author — involving 25 "healthy" football players found that creatine supplementation significantly increased serum creatinine levels. Specifically, the group who took a placebo experienced a 4.8% increase in their serum creatinine levels while the group who took creatine (15.75 grams per day for 28 days) had a 22.55% increase. The authors noted that despite the increase, the levels "remained within normal limits for individuals engaged in intense training." The fact is that those who took creatine had serum creatinine levels that were — on average — 8.7% higher than the upper limit of "normal." And if the standard deviation of the average value is considered, 16% of those who took creatine had serum creatinine levels that exceeded the upper limit of "normal" by 20%. Regardless of whether or not the increases "remained within normal limits for individuals engaged in intense training," it is clear that creatine supplementation produced a markedly greater elevation of serum creatinine levels. Along these lines, some have argued that the serum creatinine levels are elevated because creatine supposedly gives athletes the ability to train more intensely or to maintain greater training volume. This appears to be flawed thinking since the subjects in this study (who underwent the same training) did not know whether they were receiving creatine or a placebo and, therefore, would not train any differently.

Mr. Plisk stated that "short-term creatine supplementation seems to have no detrimental effect on hepatic or renal function in healthy subjects." Two points: First, any comment concerning the effects of "short-term creatine supplementation" on liver or kidney function (or anything else) is irrelevant — and not very comforting — due to the fact that the majority of individuals probably do not use creatine on a "short-term" basis. Second, his statement is not exactly true. In 1999, a previously "healthy" 20-year-old man who consumed creatine (20 grams per day for four weeks) developed nausea, vomiting and bilateral flank pain. A physical examination revealed dehydration and diffuse abdominal tenderness. The man was hospitalized and a renal biopsy found a kidney disorder known as "acute focal interstitial nephritis." This rare disorder — which occurs in roughly 1 out of 25,000 people — causes a reduction of kidney function ranging from mild dysfunction to acute kidney failure. His condition improved after he stopped taking creatine. The physicians who authored this report warned that the use of creatine may be associated with injury to the kidneys.

CAUTIONARY POSITIONS

In May 1998, the Association of Professional Team Physicians reported that 85% of its members did not recommend creatine. In June 1998, a survey published in *USA Today* revealed that only five teams in the National Football League approved the use of creatine by their players. A number of teams have written stances on creatine supplementation. For instance, the Tampa Bay Buccaneers distribute a position paper to all of their athletes that details the many potential side effects from creatine supplementation. Their position paper concludes that their organization "does not endorse creatine supplementation as a training adjunct to [their] players." It is safe to say that the reason for such cautionary positions by those entrusted with overseeing the health and safety of professional athletes is because of the potential for side effects from creatine supplementation.

But cautionary positions are not only recommended for professional athletes. In April 1999, the American College of Sports Medicine conducted an official roundtable on creatine supplementation. The roundtable — which included 12 individuals with either a doctoral or medical degree — concluded that the data on the side effects of creatine supplementation in those less than 18 years of age are "grossly inadequate" and, therefore, that it is not advised for individuals in that age group. Finally, a large number of authorities — including the Food and Drug Administration — have advised consumers not to use creatine without the approval of a physician.

THE BOTTOM LINE

Contrary to Mr. Plisk's claim, the "solid research" concerning the effectiveness of creatine supplementation on strength, endurance and lean-body mass in a laboratory setting is inconclusive. And any research that has shown an increase in strength or other performance measures cannot be generalized or applied to athletic situations that are done outside a laboratory. Indeed, the "solid research" concerning the effectiveness of creatine supplementation outside a laboratory has found that it rarely improved the performance of highly trained subjects in actual sports, realistic events or competitive situations. It is also important to note that those who would benefit the most from creatine supplementation include vegetarians and individuals with unusually low levels of creatine in their bodies.

Keep in mind, too, that studies investigating creatine are often funded by grants from supplement companies or have one or more authors who serve as "consultants" for such companies. Needless to say, it is difficult to have faith in the results of studies that have the monetary backing of companies that have a direct financial interest in the outcome of the research.

At this point in time, literally no one knows the long-term effects of creatine supplementation. Promoters of creatine supplementation insist that there are no negative side effects when it is consumed in the "recommended dosage" — typically 20-25 grams per day for 4-7 days of "loading" and then 2 grams per day for "maintenance." The unmistakable reality, however, is that the majority of individuals — thinking that "more is better" — undoubtedly exceed the "recommended dosage" of creatine on a regular basis. While on the subject, the "recommended dosage" should be relative to bodyweight. For example, a 140-pound wrestler should have a lower "recommended dosage" than a 240-pound wrestler. Finally, the potential side effects from combining creatine with one or more of the countless nutritional supplements on the market are unknown.

Mr. Plisk stated that "it may be more appropriate to compare creatine supplementation with the practice of carbohydrate loading." Perhaps in the sense that in both types of "loading," there is an attempt to "load" the stockpiles of an energy substrate. But that's where the similarities between creatine loading and carbohydrate loading end. There is really no concern with incurring any adverse side effects from consuming too many carbohydrates as there is with creatine — unless, of course, the carbohydrate loading is based upon the classical glycogen supercompensation model as proposed in the late 1960s which was found to be physiologically distressful.

Near the end of his article, Mr. Plisk advised coaches that "the student-athletes' health and well-being should be our central concern." This is truly of utmost importance. So when it comes to creatine supplementation, the bottom line for coaches and athletes is to be cautious, not careless.

BIBLIOGRAPHY

The following articles from *Wrestling USA* magazine (call 406-549-4448 for subscription information) were reprinted as chapters in this book:

Strength Training: Set Your Priorities. vol 34, no 5 (December 15, 1998): 12.

Injury Trends in Wrestling. vol 34, no 7 (February 15, 1999): 32-34.

Protecting the Knee. vol 35, no 7 (February 15, 2000): 8-9.

Protecting the Shoulder. vol 35, no 6 (January 15, 2000): 8-10.

Rehabilitative Strength Training. vol 28, no 7 (February 15, 1993): 13-14.

The Importance of Intensity. vol 24, no 7 (February 15, 1989): 6-8.

The Importance of Progressive Overload. vol 34, no 4 (November 15, 1998): 50-51.

New Perspectives in Strength. vol 23, no 3 (October 15, 1987): 18, 25-27.

10 Myths in Strength and Fitness. vol 33, no 6 (January 15, 1998): 49-50.

Coach, I Wanna Be Explosive! vol 27, no 5 (December 15, 1991): 51-53.

Adolescent Strength Training. vol 24, no 10 (April 15, 1989): 21-23.

The Trap Bar: A Productive Alternative. vol 28, no 3 (October 15, 1992): 8-9.

Strengthening the Abdominals. vol 28, no 2 (October 1, 1992): 13-15.

Neck Training: Make an EFFORT. vol 33, no 7 (February 15, 1998): 10-12.

Bench Press. vol 36, no 1 (September 15, 2000): 43-44.

Losing Fat: High or Low Intensity? vol 35, no 2 (October 1, 1999): 14-15.

Anatomy of a Stretching Program. vol 35, no 5 (December 15, 1999): 8-9.

The Safe Weight Room – Part I. vol 23, no 10 (April 15, 1988): 9-10.

The Safe Weight Room – Part II. vol 23, no 11 (May 1, 1988): 36-38.

The Creatine Myth: A Rebuttal – Part I. vol 36, no 6 (January 15, 2001): 6, 8.

The Creatine Myth: A Rebuttal – Part II. vol 36, no 7 (February 15, 2001): 6-9.

BIOGRAPHY

Matt Brzycki enlisted in the United States Marine Corps in June 1975. His active duty began two months later when he was sent to basic training (a.k.a. "boot camp") in Parris Island, South Carolina. When Mr. Brzycki completed his basic training in November 1975, he was presented the Leatherneck Award for achieving the highest score in rifle marksmanship in his platoon. In January 1978 — a little more than 28 months after beginning basic training — he was promoted meritoriously to the rank of sergeant. In May 1978, Mr. Brzycki entered Drill Instructor (DI) School at the Marine Corps Recruit Depot in San Diego, California. When he graduated from the school in August 1978 at the age of 21, he was one of the youngest DIs in the entire Marine Corps. Among his many responsibilities as a DI was the physical preparedness of Marine recruits. In August 1979, Mr. Brzycki was awarded a Certificate of Merit for successfully completing a tour of duty as a DI.

Shortly after his four-year enlistment ended in August 1979, Mr. Brzycki enrolled at Penn State. He earned a Bachelor of Science degree in Health and Physical Education in May 1983. Mr. Brzycki represented the university for two years in the Pennsylvania State Collegiate Powerlifting Championships (1981 and 1982) and was also a place-winner in his first bodybuilding competition (1981).

From May 1983-August 1984, Mr. Brzycki served as a Health Fitness Supervisor at Princeton University. In September 1984, he was named the Assistant Strength and Conditioning Coach at Rutgers University and remained in that position until July 1990. In August 1990, he returned to Princeton University as the school's Strength Coach and Health Fitness Coordinator. Mr. Brzycki was named the Coordinator of Health Fitness, Strength and Conditioning Programs in February 1994 (retroactive to December 1993). In March 2001, he was named the Coordinator of Recreational Fitness and Wellness Programming.

Over the years, Mr. Brzycki has worked with literally hundreds of male and female athletes in a wide variety of sports. Since November 1982, he has been involved in the strength and conditioning of collegiate wrestlers at three different schools: Penn State, Princeton University and Rutgers University.

Mr. Brzycki has taught at the collegiate level since 1990. He developed the Strength Training Theory and Applications course for Exercise Science and Sports Studies majors at Rutgers University and taught the program from March 1990-July 2000 as a member of the Faculty of Arts and Sciences. (Department of Exercise Science and Sport Studies.) He also taught the same course to Health and Physical Education majors at The College of New Jersey from January 1996-March 1999 as a member of the Health and Physical Education Faculty. All told, more than 600 university students in fitness-related majors took his courses in strength training for academic credit. Since September 1990, Mr. Brzycki has taught non-credit physical education courses at Princeton University including all of those pertaining to weight training.

Mr. Brzycki has been a featured speaker at local, regional, state and national conferences and clinics throughout the United States and Canada. Since November 1984, he has authored more than 200 articles on strength and fitness that have been featured in 36 different publications. Mr. Brzycki has written three books: *A Practical Approach to Strength Training* (1995), *Youth Strength and Conditioning* (1995) and *Cross Training for Fitness* (1997). He also co-authored *Conditioning for Basketball* (1993) with Shaun Brown who was, at the time, the Strength and Conditioning Coach for the University of Kentucky. (He is currently the Strength and Conditioning Coach for the Boston Celtics). Mr. Brzycki served as the editor of *Maximize your Training: Insights from Top Strength and Fitness Professionals* (1999). This 448-page book features the collective efforts of 37 leaders in the strength and fitness profession. In 1997, he developed a correspondence course in strength training for Desert Southwest Fitness (Tucson, Arizona) that is used by strength and fitness professionals to update their certifications. The course has been approved and accepted for continuing education credits by 16 international organizations including the American Council on Exercise, the Australian Fitness Advisory Council, the International Fitness Professionals Association, the International Weightlifting Association and the National Federation of Professional Trainers.

In January 2001, Mr. Brzycki was named a Fellow at Forbes College (Princeton University). In April 2001, he was selected to serve on the Alumni Society Board of Directors for the College of Health & Human Development (Penn State). He and his wife, Alicia, reside in Lawrenceville, New Jersey, with their son, Ryan.